Journey in Discipleship

STUDY GUIDE

SIXTEEN LESSONS FOR INDIVIDUAL OR GROUP STUDY

RAY PETTY

Parsons Publishing House
Christiansburg, Virginia USA

JOURNEY IN DISCIPLESHIP STUDY GUIDE
by Ray Petty

Parsons Publishing House
Christiansburg, VA 24073 USA
www.ParsonsPublishingHouse.com
Info@ParsonsPublishingHouse.com

Publisher's Note: Publisher has opted to reference satan and related names with lowercase letters.

ISBN-13: 978-1602730939
ISBN-10: 1602730938
Library of Congress Control Number: 2017908405
Printed in the United States of America.
For World-Wide Distribution.

WHAT PEOPLE ARE SAYING

This study guide is intended for use by small groups of four to eight people. It is, in my opinion, an excellent resource for this purpose. The guide is Bible-based, doctrinally sound, easy to understand, and practical. It strongly emphasizes the necessity of a personal, life-changing faith in Christ; internalizing the Word of God; and dependence on the power of the indwelling and fullness of Holy Spirit for successful Christian discipleship. Without reservation, I recommend this study guide to any who sincerely desire to "journey in discipleship," following Jesus Christ.

—Dr. Daniel L. Black, Th.D.
Editor-Writer for Pathway Press
Adult Sunday School Literature

If you are looking for a spirit-filled resource to help you grow strong disciples, you have found it. Ray Petty has poured his heart, soul, and many hours into developing this study guide. These principles are battle-tested and scripturally sound. Try it out!

—Pastor Rick Spell
Glendale UMC
Bybee, Tennessee

I have found Christians in the church are sorely lacking in the basics of the faith. Without a strong foundation they are unable to go on to maturity. Ray Petty's ***Journey in Discipleship Study Guide*** answers the need. This study is ideal for small groups. His eight essentials are not just superficial teachings; the lessons challenge us to go deeper with subjects such as assurance, forgiveness, God's Word, and prayer. They answer the heartfelt struggles people have with doubt, guilt, loneliness and self-sufficiency, purpose, and the keys to transformation. Ray has the ability to ask the right questions and give solid scriptural answers. He takes us from understanding these truths to applying them in our lives with very practical steps. This is a study that will transform lives.

—Doug Wilder
Rutherford Memorial UMC
Corryton, Tennessee

TABLE OF CONTENTS

INTRODUCTION

How To Use This Material

> And He Himself gave some to be apostles, some prophets, some evangelists, and some pastors and teachers, for the equipping of the saints for the work of ministry, for the edifying of the body of Christ (Ephesians 4:11-12).

This is the instruction from the apostle Paul concerning the job description for those in leadership. This is also a mandate God gives to the church to go and make disciples. The message of the Good News of Jesus Christ never changes, only the methods of how we reach others change. I believe that it is important to fulfill the call of God and to seek how we as a church must find effective ways to reach others for the purpose of making more and better disciples.

There are four major ingredients for a healthy church:

- Love
- Community/fellowship
- Mission/outreach
- Equipping/instruction

The way that best fulfills these ingredients is through small groups of eight to twelve people meeting together on a regular basis outside the church for the purpose of building relationships, reaching out to others, making disciples, and leadership development, with the goal of multiplication. Small groups are life-giving and take Christ into the community to transform the world.

Journey in Discipleship Study Guide helps to prepare for this purpose:

- To assist individuals to grow and mature in their walk and relationship to Jesus Christ.
- To prepare and train facilitators to lead the small groups.
- To equip individuals for effective service and ministry in the church.
- To assist people to discover and know their spiritual gifts.

How does *Journey in Discipleship Study Guide* work?

The participants have an opportunity to meet together for sixteen weeks for discussion, application, prayer, fellowship, and equipping.

Each session should begin with sharing how the week has gone since your last meeting together, prayer by inviting the Holy Spirit to guide your time together, and to give everyone opportunity to share their responses to the questions. This is an equipping and discussion time each week. It is a sharing time of what God has shown you about the lesson and allowing the Holy Spirit to apply these truths and principles to your life.

The person facilitating can observe the 70/30 principle: to speak 30% of the time and listen 70% of the time (with some equipping time included). Close your time together by praying for one another asking God to apply the things the Holy Spirit has shown you about that lesson. Finally, review the commitments for ***Journey in Discipleship Study Guide***.

This book is a paradigm of how to make disciples for the transformation of the world. It will help the church to be more fruitful, more Christ-like, and more intentional about how and why we do church the way we do. It assists us to move from being meeting-centered, to people making disciples.

What makes *Journey in Discipleship Study Guide* different?

- We have a cause—to fulfill the ministry of Jesus.
- We have a plan—to make every believer a minister.
- We have a method—to equip and to serve.
- We have a promise—Jesus said, "Follow Me and I will make you fishers of men."

The multiplication of small groups is the single most important element of every healthy small group ministry that has longevity. From the beginning the DNA of your small group system must hinge on the multiplication of every small group. Failure to understand this step is usually fatal to any small group system.

—Bill Easum and John Atkinson
Authors of ***Go Big With Small Groups***

Section One

JOURNEY IN DISCIPLESHIP

The Essentials

LESSON 1

THE JOURNEY BEGINS

Objective The objective of this lesson is to experience the confident assurance of our salvation, to know God's purpose and plan for our lives, and to lead others into that same assurance.

> These things I have written to you who believe in the name of the Son of God, that you may know [through personal experience] that you have eternal life, and that you may continue to believe in the name of the Son of God (1 John 5:13).

This lesson keys in on how we can walk with an assurance of our salvation, our identity in Christ, and how we can live an overcoming life because Christ in us is our hope for glory in this life as well as in the life to come. Isaiah declares, "Arise, shine; for your light has come! And the glory of the Lord is risen upon you" (Isaiah 60:1). We can rise out of our doubts, fears, and darkness. For Jesus, our Light has come and His glory has filled us, "for we have beheld His glory, glory as the only begotten of the Father full of grace and truth" (John 1:14).

We are in this world and called to be light, declare where darkness is to be light, and to demonstrate that greater is He who is in us than he who is in the world (1 John 4:2). The light of Christ in us penetrates the darkness of this world so we can demonstrate the transformed life we have in the person of Jesus Christ.

> Ask the Father to show you areas in your life where He desires to bring healing and wholeness. Those areas need His unconditional love to heal hurts and wounds you have experienced. Ask for the love of God to be spread abroad in your heart by the Holy Spirit (Romans 5:5).

I declare this will be a time when God does something powerful and transformational in your life. May this be a time of new beginnings and renewed love for the Savior.

I believe all Christians want to know they will be received into heaven as they hear these hope-filled words of our heavenly Father, "Well done, good and faithful servant... Enter into the joy of your Lord" (Matthew 25:21). This promise begins right now.

What is our assurance based on?

> For by grace you have been saved through faith (right believing leads to right living), and that not of yourselves; it is the gift of God, not of works, lest anyone should boast (Ephesians 2:8-9).

Mark the one that our assurance is based upon:

☐ Our feelings

☐ Our knowledge of the Bible

☐ Our service to others

☐ Our prayer life

☐ Our faith

Why do many Christians not have an assurance of their salvation?

Some reasons include: they hope they have been good enough to spend eternity with God, they feel they need to earn God's favor to enter into heaven, or possibly they have not experienced the truth of God's Word for themselves. However, we CAN have assurance for our salvation:

- We have the assurance of God's Word which says, "Who has saved us and called us with a holy calling, not according to our works, but according to His own purpose and grace which was given to us in Christ Jesus before time began" (2 Timothy 1:9).
- We have the assurance of the witness of the Spirit in Romans 8:16, "The Spirit Himself bears

witness with our spirit that we are children of God."

- We have the assurance of a transformed life in a verse that reads, "Therefore, if anyone is in Christ, he is a new creation; old things have passed away; behold, all things become new" (2 Corinthians 5:17).
- We have the assurance of freedom in Christ as seen in 2 Corinthians 3:17, "Now the Lord is the Spirit; and where the Spirit of the Lord is, there is liberty."

This is a promise for those in the household of faith: "But as many as receive Him, to them **He gave the right** to become children of God, to those who believe in His name" (John 1:12, emphasis added).

What do we become when we receive Christ?

God's Word says, "Who has saved us and called us with a holy calling, not according to our works, but according to His own purpose and grace which was given to us in Christ Jesus before time began" (2 Timothy 1:9).

Three reasons why we need Christ:

1 Because we have a past.

"For all have sinned and fallen short of the glory of God" (Romans 3:23).

John the Baptist had to come to grips with His own testimony when he saw the heavens open and the Spirit of God rested upon Jesus in the form of a dove (John 1:32). We must come to our own experience that Jesus is the One who takes away the sin of the world—even mine. We cannot declare what we do not know. John was watching Jesus come toward him and says, "Behold! The Lamb of God who **takes away** the **sin** of the world" (John 1:29). This became John's personal testimony that he would be able to share with his disciples and with the whole world to point them to Jesus.

> The word "sin" (*hamartia*) means to "miss the mark, taking the wrong course."
>
> The phrase "takes away" means to remove, to carry off, to take up.

Jeremiah declares God's will: "For I will forgive their sin, and their sin I will remember no more" (Jeremiah 31:34).

? Why can we live as a forgiven person?

Jesus said, "Therefore if the Son **makes you free,** you shall be free indeed" (John 8:36). God's unmerited favor keeps us hitting the mark and guards us from missing the mark.

> The phrase "makes you free" means to deliver, to set free. Jesus frees us from the dominion and power of sin.
>
> Begin to declare over your life, "I am a forgiven person because Christ has forgiven me of all my sins" (Colossians 2:13).

2 **Because we have a friend.** "No longer do I call you servants, for a servant does not know what His master is doing; but I call you friends, for all things that I heard from My Father I have made known to you" (John 15:15). God's promise to anyone who comes to Him, "will by no means cast out" (John 6:37). Jesus calls us into a friendship relationship.

3 **Because of God's plan for our lives.** "For I know the plans I have for you, declares the Lord, "plans to prosper you and not to harm you, plans to give you hope and a future" (Jeremiah 29:11, NIV). God gives purpose to our lives and imparts His life-giving Spirit.

> What is God's plan for you?

What does assurance give us?

- Peace about our past and the joy of Christ in us.
- Confidence to come boldly into the presence of God.
- Victory over sin and its dominion in our lives.
- Confidence that we can walk in God's purpose and plan for our lives.
- A knowing that we are sons and daughters of God.
- We stand totally forgiven, completely accepted, and unconditionally loved.

? Which one of the statements about assurance spoke to you the most and why?

! **The key to assurance is resting in the finished work of Jesus on the cross and adding nothing to it.**

God's Word Gives Us Assurance

- **We have the assurance of God's presence** as seen in this passage:

For God Himself has said, I will not in any way fail you nor give you up nor leave you with without support. [I will] not. [I will] not, [I will] not in any degree leave you helpless, nor

> forsake nor let [you] down, [relax My hold on you].—Assuredly not! (Hebrews 13:5, AMP).

There is only one thing that is necessary for the believer and that is the presence of God. When God was leading the people of Israel through the wilderness into the Promised Land, the one thing Moses desired was that the presence of God would accompany them on their journey (Exodus 33:14).

- **We have the assurance that God is still working on us.**

> And I am convinced and sure of this very thing, that He who began a good work in you will continue until the day of Jesus Christ—right up to the time of His return—developing [that good work] and perfecting and bringing it to full completion in you (Philippians 1:6, AMP).

God is still working in our lives. We are not the completed product. Therefore, we can trust Him that He does all things well (Mark 7:37).

- **We have the assurance that our sins are forgiven.**

> And when you were dead in your transgressions...He made you alive together with Him, having forgiven us all our transgressions (Colossians 2:13).

"I, even I, am He who blots out your transgressions for My own sake; and I will not remember your sins" (Isaiah 43:25).

We live as forgiven people (past, present, and future). We enjoy forgiveness because of Jesus' death on the cross and we stand forgiven on this side of the cross.

- **We have the assurance of God's unconditional love.**

"The Lord has appeared of old to me saying, 'Yes, I have loved you; therefore with lovingkindness I have drawn you'" (Jeremiah 31:3).

> For I am persuaded that neither death nor life, nor angels nor principalities nor powers, nor things present nor things to come, nor height nor depth, nor any other created thing, shall be able to separate us from the love of God which is in Christ Jesus our Lord (Romans 8:38-39).

God loves everyone; He loves the world. He loves you, and you can live as a person deeply loved by God. He is not disappointed in you, but draws you to Himself to affirm you, to embrace you, and to lavish His love upon you. His love is not based on our merit or good works; it's based on His grace and kindness.

- **We have the assurance of God's power to make us victorious in life as over comers.**

> Who shall separate us from the love of Christ? Shall tribulation, or distress, or persecution, or famine, or nakedness, or peril, or sword? Yet in all these things we are more than conquerors through Him who loved us (Romans 8:35, 37).

The apostle Paul writes, "But thanks be to God, who gives us the victory through our Lord Jesus Christ" (1 Corinthians 15:57). Through the life, death, and resurrection of Jesus we are seated with Him in heavenly places, and we are victorious, overcoming, and triumphant in and through the person of Jesus Christ (Ephesians 1:20-22, 2:6)

Which one of the five statements about assurance spoke to you the most and why?

Our prayer is:

Father, I ask that You would fill my heart with the assurance of Your love, affection, and kindness You have for me. I ask that You would remove all guilt, shame, doubt, fears, and any other things that would keep me from experiencing the joy of Your presence and Your overwhelming love for me. I accept the unconditional kindness, love, and affection You have for me. I receive Your freedom to walk in the assurance that I belong to You and that nothing can take that away. Amen!

Group Discussion and Application

Sharing:

How did it go this week? (A time of informal sharing)

Opening prayer inviting the Holy Spirit to guide your time together

Walking Through the Lesson:

- Take time to review the lesson for this week and go over any questions that the group might have.
- Describe one thing you learned from this lesson.
- What challenged you the most about this lesson?
- Where does our assurance come from and what is the basis for our assurance?
- What is significant about God loving us even before we knew or even cared about Him?
- How has this lesson given you a greater assurance about your relationship to Jesus Christ? Do you

have a greater assurance of God's purpose and plan for your life?

- You might want to give everyone an opportunity to share what assurance means to them and how they came to have God's assurance in their lives or if they are still struggling with this.

- Be sure to end with a time of praying for one another about having an assurance of who they are in Christ and His plan and purpose for their lives.

Our Four Commitments:

- To complete the lesson each week and be ready to share what you learned.
- To let someone in the group know if you are unable to attend the meeting.
- To pray for one another on a regular basis throughout the week.
- To ask God what He is calling you to do about making disciples through building relationships, reaching out to others, and multiplying through small groups.

LESSON 2

THE ROAD THAT LEADS TO FREEDOM

Objective To experience God's unconditional love, acceptance, and forgiveness; to walk in love and to give it away; and to lead others through the steps of forgiveness.

"He is so rich in kindness that He purchased our freedom through the blood of His Son, and our sins are forgiven" (Ephesians 1:7, NLT).

God's gift to us is His forgiveness. Jesus gave His life so that we could experience forgiveness and live as forgiven people. Our response to God's forgiveness is to receive this gift for there is no more condemnation to those who are in Christ Jesus (Romans 8:1). When we live as forgiven people, we can walk in forgiveness and give it away, and we can enjoy God's freedom of no condemnation.

Put a check beside the statement that describes why we are forgiven:

□Because we live a good moral life.
□Because we are members of a local church.
□Because the blood of Christ frees us from sin's power.

Forgiveness means the release from bondage or imprisonment, with the added quality of canceling out all judgment, punishment or debt (read Colossians 2:13-14). John 19:30 record the words of Jesus from the cross to His heavenly Father, "it is finished.

The word "finished" *(tetelestai)* means paid in full. This is what Jesus did to our sin—paid it in full with His life.

What is God's promise to us about our sins?

Experiencing God's Forgiveness

"If we confess our sins, He is faithful and just to forgive us our sins and to cleanse us from all unrighteousness" (1 John 1:9). The Psalmist declared:

> When I refused to confess my sin, I was weak and miserable, and I groaned all day long. Day

> and night your hand of discipline was heavy on me. My strength evaporated like water in the summer heat. Finally, I confessed all my sins to you and stopped trying to hide them. I said, 'I will confess my rebellion to the Lord.' And You forgave me! All my guilt is gone" (Psalm 32:3-5, NLT).

? Briefly describe what happened to David when he was honest about his sin.

The Psalmist states:

> Create in me a clean heart, O God. Renew a right spirit within me. Do not banish me from Your presence, and don't take Your Holy Spirit from me. Restore to me again the joy of Your salvation, and make me willing to obey You" (Psalm 51: 10-12, NLT).

? How can we experience healing through forgiveness?

We receive healing, freedom, health, vitality, and oppression lifts when we allow the Lord to deal with the deep things of the heart and we enter into the joy of the Lord.

Why we can experience God's forgiveness

"For all have sinned; all fall short of God's glorious standard" (Romans 3:23, NLT).

> But if we are living in the light of God's presence, just as Christ is, then we have fellowship with each other, and the blood of Jesus, His Son, cleanses us from every sin (1 John 1:7, NLT).

"He has sent me to heal (make whole) the brokenhearted" (Isaiah 61:1).

> "Come now, and let us reason together," says the Lord. "Though your sins are like scarlet, they shall be as white as snow; though they are red like crimson, they shall be as wool" (Isaiah 1:18).

? From these verses of Scripture describe how we can experience God's forgiveness.

Let's summarize the above verses that speak of our need for God's forgiveness:

- All have missed God's best for our lives and need His forgiveness.
- The way to walk in fellowship with God and with others is to receive His forgiveness.
- We need to know that God forgets and doesn't hold our sins over our heads.
- God's forgiveness brings wholeness and healing to our lives from sin's destructive patterns.
- No matter what we have done, we find in Christ His cleansing, His freedom, and our transformation from sin's power through God's forgiveness.

Why is it important to apply God's forgiveness to others?

The apostle Paul writes, "And be kind to one another, tenderhearted, forgiving one another, even as God in Christ forgave you" (Ephesians 4:32). Jesus said, "If you have anything against anyone, forgive him that your Father in heaven may also forgive you your trespasses" (Mark 11:25). James writes, "Confess your sins to one another, and pray for one another, that you may be healed" (James 5:16).

Forgiveness is an act of the will. It is a decision we make to walk in forgiveness and to give it away. Forgiveness is our gift that we give to others who offend us, speak ill of us, and who hold grudges against us. We forgive them, release them, and bless them. It is the way of health and healing, and walking in the fullness of Christ. It is giving

Him away to those who need to experience His love and forgiveness.

> How can we walk in forgiveness and give it away?

Walking Out of Bitterness into Freedom

What is forgiveness?

- **Forgiveness is God's command.**

  For if you forgive men their trespasses, your heavenly Father will also forgive you. But if you do not forgive men their trespasses, neither will your Father forgive your trespasses (Matthew 6:14-15).

God's command is our invitation to walk in love and to give it away. God's command is our opportunity to practice discipleship. God's command is showing the kindness of Christ.

- **Forgiveness is necessary to avoid entrapment by Satan.**

> Now whom you forgive anything, I also forgive. For if indeed I have forgiven anything. I have forgiven that one for your sakes in the presence of Christ. Lest Satan should take advantage of us; for we are not ignorant of his devices (2 Corinthians 2:10-11).

Forgiveness closes the door on satan from gaining entrance into our hearts. We must close any door of unforgiveness by forgiving others.

- **Forgiveness is required of all believers who desire to be like Christ.**

> And do not grieve the Holy Spirit of God, by whom you were sealed for the day of redemption. Let all bitterness, wrath, anger, clamor, and evil speaking be put away from you, with all malice. And be kind to one another, tenderhearted, forgiving one another, even as Christ forgave you (Ephesians 4:31-32).

Walking in forgiveness shows that Christ is Lord of our lives and demonstrates a Christ-like Spirit. Our desire is to be like Christ in all things as He lives His life through us.

> Bearing with one another, and forgiving one another, if anyone has a complaint against another; even as Christ forgave you, so you also must do (Colossians 3:13).

- **Forgiveness is the way to freedom.**

Forgiveness assures us that we are walking in our freedom in Christ. Holding on to grudges, bitterness, and anger causes a spiritual logjam and stops the flow of the Holy Spirit. Forgiveness is a must if we want to enjoy our freedom in Christ.

We may not be able to forgive, but God can and that may be the statement we say over and over again toward our freedom in Christ. In our weakness God's grace can give us strength to forgive (2 Corinthians 12:9). The only real choice is to live with the consequences in the bondage of bitterness or in the freedom of forgiveness. If you bury your feelings, you will bypass the possibility of forgiveness; you must forgive from the heart.

- **Forgiveness is the way to health and healing.**

"Fear the Lord and depart from evil. It will be health to your flesh, and strength to your bones" (Proverbs 3:7b-8).

> When I kept silent, my bones grew old through my groaning all the day long. For day and night Your hand was heavy upon me; my vitality was turned into the drought of summer. I acknowledged my sin to You and my iniquity I have not hidden. I said, "I will confess my transgressions to the Lord." And You forgave the iniquity of my sin (Psalm 32:3-5).

"Who forgives all your iniquities and heals all your diseases" (Psalm 103:3).

Forgiveness is the way to health and healing. Anger, resentment, and bitterness cause side affects—sickness, disease, and mental fatigue. We must guard our hearts if we desire to walk in health and healing. If you are experiencing sickness, do a spiritual inventory on forgiveness.

- **Forgiveness demonstrates the <u>Lordship</u> of Jesus in our lives.**

  Then Peter came to Him and said, "Lord, how often shall my brother sin against me, and I forgive him? Up to seven times?" Jesus said to him, "I do not say to you up to seven times, but up to seventy times seven" (Matthew 18:21-22).

? What does it mean to you to walk in total forgiveness?

"Forgiveness is good news because it opens the way to the enjoyment of God himself."—John Piper

Forgiveness is:

- **Learning to forget.** Forgetting may be a long-term by-product of forgiving. God says He will not remember our sins, "Their sins and their lawless deeds I will remember no more" (Hebrews 10:17).

- **Not tolerating future sin.** It is okay to forgive another's past sin and at the same time, take a stand against future sins.

- **Not seeking revenge or demand payment for offenses suffered.** "Beloved, do not avenge yourselves, but rather give place to wrath; for it is written, 'vengeance is Mine, I will repay,' says the Lord" (Romans 12:19).

Steps to Forgiveness:

- Ask the Lord to bring to your mind the people you need to forgive. Write on a sheet of paper the names of these who offended you. (Father, mother, spouse, relative, co-worker, God, yourself)
- Acknowledge the hurt. State specifically for what you are forgiving them (rejection, deprivation of love, unfairness, verbal, sexual, emotional abuse, betrayal, or neglect).
- Understand the sacrifice of the cross. Jesus took upon Himself all the sins of the world—including yours and those of the person who has offended you. He died "once for all" (Hebrews 10:10).
- Decide to forgive. Forgiveness is a crisis of the will—a conscious choice to let the other person off the hook and to free yourself from the past. Your

feelings of forgiveness will follow in time. Don't say, "I want to forgive so and so," or "Lord help me to forgive so and so." That's bypassing your responsibility and choice to forgive.

- Take your list to God and pray the following, "I forgive (name) for (list all the offenses and how they made you feel)." Stay with each person on the list until every remembered pain has been specifically addressed.
- Destroy the list. You are now free. Do not tell the offenders what you have done. Your freedom in Christ cannot be dependent upon others whom you have no control over.
- Do not expect that your decision to forgive will result in major changes in the other person. Instead, pray for them (Matthew 5:44) so they too may find the freedom of forgiveness (2 Corinthians 2:7). Thank God for the lessons you have learned and the maturity you have found as a result of your decision to forgive the offenders (Romans 8:28, 29).

Our prayer is:

Father, I receive Your unconditional love and acceptance. I ask Your forgiveness for the anger, resentment, and hurts I have held on to. I release to You all my hurts and offenses that I have taken toward others and the judgments I have made about others. Father, I forgive, release, and bless those who have offended me in any way. Father, I want Your freedom more than my bondage that separates me from You and from others. Father, thank You for Your forgiveness; I receive Your forgiveness and I forgive myself. In Jesus' name, Amen!

Group Discussion and Application

Sharing:

How did it go this week?

Opening prayer inviting the Holy Spirit to guide our time together

Walking Through the Lesson:

- Describe one thing you learned from this lesson.
- What challenged you the most about this lesson?
- According to our lesson, what is sin and what does it do?
- How did God deal with our sin?
- What is the basis of our forgiveness?
- Describe a time you experienced the forgiveness of God. What did it feel like, and what happened as a result of that forgiveness?

- How can we experience Christ's freedom? What would it take for that to happen?

Make sure you understand and claim "The Steps to Forgiveness" found in this section as your own personal prayer.

> Forgiveness means not merely that I am saved from Hell and made right for heaven; forgiveness means that I am forgiven into a recreated relationship, into identification with God in Christ.
>
> —Oswald Chambers,
> ***My Utmost for His Highest***

Our Four Commitments:

- To complete the lesson each week and be ready to share what you learned.
- To let someone in the group know if you are unable to attend the meeting.
- To pray for one another on a regular basis throughout the week.
- To ask God what He is calling you to do about making disciples through building relationships, reaching out to others, and multiplying through small groups.

LESSON 3

RECEIVING POWER FOR THE JOURNEY

Objective To experience God's power in our lives and be able to assist others to encounter the power of God in their lives also.

Word Study for God's Power

Jesus said we would have this authority: "And to have power *(exousia)* to heal sickness and to cast out demons" (Mark 3:15).

> Greek word for "power" is *exousia* meaning authority, or right to act, ability, capacity, delegated authority. "And He called them to Himself, and began to send them out two by two, and gave them power *(exousia)* over unclean spirits" (Mark 6:7).

The disciples ministered in the name of Jesus, "And with great power *(dunamis)* the apostles gave witness to the resurrection of the Lord Jesus. And great grace was upon them all" (Acts 4:33).

> Greek word for "power" is *dunamis* meaning energy, power, might, great force, great ability.

One of the names of God is *El Shaddai* meaning God Almighty. To Abraham God said, "I am Almighty God; walk before Me and be blameless" (Genesis 17:1).

> *El Shaddai* means mighty, unconquerable, greatness, strength, or His everlasting nature. He is an all-sufficient God, eternally capable of being all that His people need.

God's Word is alive and active (Hebrews 4:12). We can feed upon the Word of God that nourishes our spirits, encourages us in our minds, conforms us to His will, and causes us to feel what Christ feels. We can declare God's Word over our lives and claim His promises for everything in life.

Let the Word of God dwell richly within you (Colossians 3:16). Mediate upon His Word and let it bear fruit that last forever. This lesson is how the Word of God gives us access to the promises of God, the provision of God, and the power of God.

How Scripture Speaks of the Power of God

God is called All-Powerful. "God spoke once, twice I have heard this: that power belongs to God" (Psalm 62:11).

A. His power can be:

- **Seen (visible)** – "So I looked for You in the sanctuary, to see Your power and Your glory" (Psalm 63:2). "That He would grant you, according to the riches of His glory, to be strengthened with might [power, *dunamis*] through His Spirit in the inner man" (Ephesians 3:16).
- **Felt** – "The voice of the Lord is powerful; the voice of the Lord is full of majesty" (Psalm 29:4). We might say, "I felt His presence."
- **Experienced** – "To know the love of Christ which passes knowledge; that you may be filled with all the fullness of God" (Ephesians 3:19).

We see the power of God in creation. We see the power of God working in our lives and in the lives of others. We see God's power at work in bringing circumstances to work together for His glory and for our good. We see the great need for the power of God at work on our behalf, making us more than conquerors through His Son, Jesus.

B. God's Power has the ability:

- **To transform us.** "For I am not ashamed of the gospel of Christ, for it is the power [*dunamis*] of God to salvation for everyone who believes" (Romans 1:16).
- **To empower us for ministry and service.** "But you shall receive power [*dunamis*] when the Holy Spirit has come upon you..." (Acts 1:8).
- **To equip us for an overcoming life.** "As His divine power [*dunamis*] has given to us all things that pertain to life and godliness..." (2 Peter 1:3).

- **To manifest Himself through us.** "Behold, I send the Promise of My Father upon you; but tarry in the city of Jerusalem until you are endued with power [*dunamis*] from on high" (Luke 24:49).
- **To change circumstances.** "Then He came and touched the open coffin, and those who carried him stood still. And He said, 'Young man, I say to you, arise'" (Luke 7:14). The folks responded by saying, "God has visited His people" (Luke 7:16).
- **To heal us.** "And the whole multitude sought to touch Him, for power [*dunamis*] went out from Him and healed them all" (Luke 6:19).
- **To set us free.** "For God has not given us a spirit of fear, but of power and of love and of a sound mind" (2 Timothy 1:7). "He gives power to the weak, and to those who have no might, He increases strength" (Isaiah 40:29).
- **To make us more than conquerors/victorious.**

  My grace is sufficient for you, for my strength is made perfect in weakness. Therefore most gladly I will rather boast in my infirmities, that the power [*dunamis*] of Christ may rest upon me (2 Corinthians 12:9).

? From the above eight ways that we can experience the power of God, which one spoke to you the most and why?

God's power at work:

> Nevertheless He saved them for His name's sake, that He might make His mighty power known. He rebuked the Red Sea also, and it dried up; so He led them through the depths, as through the wilderness. He saved them from the hand of him who hated them, and redeemed them from the hand of the enemy (Psalm 106:8-10).

Paul writes, "And my speech and my preaching were not with persuasive words of human wisdom, but in demonstration of the Spirit and of power" (1 Corinthians 2:4).

> ? How or in what ways is the power of God demonstrated?

God's power gives us new life.

"For I am not ashamed of the gospel of Christ, for it is the power of God to salvation for everyone who believes" (Romans 1:16).

"For the message of the cross is foolishness to those who are perishing, but to us who are being saved it is the power of God" (1 Corinthians 1:18).

"That I may know Him and the power of His resurrection" (Philippians 3:10).

> But if the Spirit who raised Jesus from the dead dwells in you, He who raised Christ from the dead will also give life to your mortal bodies through His Spirit who dwells in you (Romans 8:11).

? Why do we need the power of God in our lives?

Why We Need to be Filled with God's Power

- **To receive God's gift:**
  Repent, and receive the gift of the Holy Spirit. For the promise is to you and to your children, and to all who are afar off, as many as the Lord our God will call (Acts 2:38-39).

> How do we receive the gift of the Holy Spirit, and to whom is it given?

- **To receive God's love:**

"Now hope does not disappoint, because the love of God has been poured out in our hearts by the Holy Spirit who was given to us" (Romans 5:5).

> What happens when we are filled with God's Spirit?

- **To be witnesses:**

  But you shall receive power when the Holy Spirit has come upon you; and you shall be witnesses to Me in Jerusalem, and in all Judea and Samaria, and to the end of the earth (Acts 1:8).

"With great power the apostles gave witness to the resurrection of the Lord Jesus. And great grace was upon them all" (Acts 4:33).

> And when they had prayed, the place where they were assembled together was shaken; and they were all filled with the Holy Spirit, and they spoke the word of God with boldness (Acts 4:31).

Why has the Holy Spirit been given and how do we receive the Spirit's power?

- **To activate the gifts of the Holy Spirit:**

> Having then gifts differing according to the grace that is given to us, let us use them: if prophesy, let us prophesy in proportion to our faith; or ministry, let us use it in our ministering; he who teaches, in teaching; he who exhorts, in exhortation; he who gives, with liberality; he who leads, with diligence; he who shows mercy, with cheerfulness (Romans 12:6-8).

How are the gifts of the Spirit given? Why is it important to know what our spiritual gift is? Do you know what your spiritual gift is?

Steps to Being Filled with God's Spirit

"Do not be drunk with wine, which leads to debauchery. Instead be filled with the Spirit" (Ephesians 5:18).

The phrase "be filled" means to be continuously filled with the Spirit of God in such a way that there is room for nothing else but God's Spirit as we make ourselves available to Him.

- **Ask** God to fill you with His Spirit (Luke 11:13).
- By faith **receive** the gift of the Spirit into your life (Mark 11:24).
- Begin to **declare and demonstrate** the Spirit's power as you walk in love, as you discover and use your spiritual gift, and as you witness to God's grace and mercy (Romans 5:5, 12:6-8; Acts 4:31-33). We are to encourage others to be filled with God's Spirit (1 Corinthians 14:3).

The word "gift" charisma is defined as God's grace, free gift, spiritual endowment, that is used in the Body of Christ for encouragement, exhortation, and comfort (1 Corinthians 14:3).

Our prayer is:

Father, I ask that You would fill me with Your Holy Spirit. I ask that You would flood my heart with Your overwhelming love. I believe that as I ask, You are filling me with Your Spirit, and I receive everything You desire to give me. I ask that Your Spirit would be like fuel to my spirit igniting it with Your power. Father, I open myself to You and to Your life-giving Spirit to be a witness to Your transforming power. Come Holy Spirit! In Jesus' name, Amen!

Group Discussion and Application

Sharing:

How did it go this week?

Opening prayer inviting the Holy Spirit to guide our time together

Walking Through the Lesson:

- Describe one thing you learned from this lesson.
- What challenged you the most about this lesson?
- What is God's command about being filled with the Spirit, and why is it essential to be filled with the Holy Spirit?
- Describe a time you experienced the power of God in your life. What would happen if we lived the Spirit-filled life?
- What difference do you think being filled with God's Spirit will make in your life?
- What difference would it make in the life of the church if we invited the Holy Spirit to be in our midst?

- Pray for one another to be filled with the Holy Spirit.

> We need a vision of a Church made up of transformed believers who are filled with the Spirit, obedient to His leading, and who may properly be called "disciples." We need a church filled with believers who have put aside all bondages and "besetting sins" and who are living victorious lives.
>
> —Randy Clark
> ***Power, Holiness and Evangelism***

Our Four Commitments:

- To complete the lesson for each week and be ready to share what you learned.
- To let someone in the group know if you are unable to attend the meeting.
- To pray for one another on a regular basis.
- To ask God what He is calling you to do about making disciples through building relationships, reaching out to others, and multiplying through small groups.

LESSON 4

LIFE TOGETHER ON THE JOURNEY

Objective To cultivate an abiding relationship with Jesus that impacts my fellowship with believers and to encourage others to build similar relationships.

> Word Study:
> Fellowship (*koinonia*) means sharing, unity, close association, partnership. Fellowship (*koinonia*) cements the believers to the Lord Jesus and to each other.

Joe Ellis, in his book ***The Church on Purpose,*** observes, "Christian fellowship is fragile. It requires patience to develop and care to maintain. Churches must consciously and consistently work to strengthen this quality among its people." John in his epistle writes, "If we walk in the light as He is in the light, we have fellowship with one another" (1 John 1:7).

Howard Snyder, in his book ***The Problem of Wine Skins,*** explains, "Two dimensions of fellowship must be understood: the vertical dimension of the believer's fellowship with God and the horizontal dimension of his fellowship with other believers through the Holy Spirit." He concludes by saying, "It is my conviction that the *koinonia* of the Holy Spirit is most likely to be experienced when Christians meet together informally in small-group fellowships."

Larry Crabb observes:

> I speak of spiritual community as a gathering of people who experience a kind of togetherness that only the Holy Spirit makes possible...at its core, the church is a spiritual community journeying together toward God." He goes on to say, "If we are going to walk with God, one thing is immediately clear: we must go in the same direction. And God doesn't negotiate. He invites us to join Him. He will not go with us on our side trips (***Finding God***).

Which one of these quotes spoke to you the most and why?

Scripture tells us why we are to walk in unity:

- It begins with our **walk** with God. "And Enoch walked with God; and he was not, for God took him" (Genesis 5:24). When I am walking in relationship to Christ, in fellowship with Him, then I can walk in fellowship with others in the Body of Christ.
- We **experience** the nature and character of God. Jesus prayed, "...That they all may be one, as You, Father, are in Me, and I in You; that they also may be one in Us, that the world may believe that You sent Me" (John 17:21).
- It is an environment, a **culture** we seek to cultivate. Unity is the result of God's people being filled with His Spirit and speaking the same thing. Ephesians 5:18-19 says, "But be filled with Spirit, speaking to one another..."
- It is the place where God pours out **blessing**, He touches us from the top of our head to soles of our feet. "And the Lord has pronounced His blessing, even life for evermore" (Psalm 133:3). **Unity** is cooperating with the prayer of Jesus. The purpose for cultivating an environment of unity is for the "strengthening of the church" (1 Corinthians 14:26).

Why has God commanded blessing where there is unity?

In order to appreciate unity, we must understand what disunity will do when there is not shared vision, mission, purpose, and values.

- When we demand our way, unity and creativity are stifled—we are not at our best.
- When we become critical, the church becomes anemic—we lose our strength and our testimony begins to wane.
- When we have more than one vision, it creates division (two visions). We are not walking together to fulfill the purpose of God. We forget why we exist.
- When we have us (long timers) vs. them (new folks), this is rooted in a fear that the Lord will take the church in a way we have never been before or in a way in which we are not comfortable.
- Therefore, division "grieves the Spirit of God" (1 Thessalonians 5:19) and will "quench the Spirit's fire" (Ephesians 4:30). "Make every effort to keep the unity of the Spirit through the bond of peace" (Ephesians 4:3).

Philippians 2:1-2 says:

> Therefore if there is any encouragement in Christ, if any comfort of love, if any fellowship of the Spirit, if any affection and mercy, fulfill my joy by being likeminded, having the same love, being of one accord, of one mind.

According to Philippians 2:1-2 how does Paul describe Christian community?

Now all who believed were together, and had all things in common, and sold their possessions and goods, and divided them among all, as anyone had need. So continuing daily with one accord in the temple, and breaking bread from house to house, they ate their food with gladness and simplicity of heart, praising God and having favor with all the people. And the Lord added to the church daily those who were being saved (Acts 2:44-47).

How and where did evangelism take place according to Acts 2:44-47? How can small groups help in building community?

The purpose of fellowship:

> And let us consider one another in order to stir up love and good works, not forsaking the assembling of ourselves together, as is the manner of some, but exhorting one another, and so much the more as you see the Day approaching (Hebrews 10:24-25).

According to Hebrews 10:24-25 what happens when the church comes together?

God did not call us to be "lone-rangers." He called us into community—into relationship. God called us to be a part of something larger than ourselves—the Christian community.

Building Christian Community

> Let each one of you speak truth with his neighbor, for we are members of one another. Be angry, and do not sin; do not let the sun go down on your wrath, nor give place to the devil...Let no corrupt word proceed out of your mouth, but what is good for necessary

> edification, that it may impart grace to the hearers. And do not grieve the Holy Spirit of God, by whom you were sealed for the day of redemption. Let all bitterness wrath, anger, quarreling, and evil speaking be put away from you...And be kind to one another, tenderhearted, forgiving one another, even as God in Christ forgave you (Ephesians 4:25-32).

? How can we grieve the Holy Spirit?

Cultivating a dynamic fellowship with Jesus Christ:

"God is faithful, by whom you were called into the fellowship of His Son, Jesus Christ" (1 Corinthians 1:9). "Abide in Me, and I in you. As the branch cannot bear fruit of itself, unless it abides in the vine, neither can you, unless you abide in Me" (John 15:4).

? What has the believer been called to do? What is the key to living a fruitful life?

Our prayer is:

Father, my desire is to walk in fellowship with Your Son, Jesus. Help me as I seek to do that. I ask that You would remove any barrier that would keep me from walking in fellowship with You and with others. Forgive me for any barriers I have put up that would keep me from walking in authentic fellowship with You and with others. Father, show me how to build bridges and connect with my brothers and sisters in Christ in a way that makes a difference in me and in the community around me. In Jesus' name, Amen!

Group Discussion and Application

Sharing:

How did it go this week?

Opening prayer inviting the Holy Spirit to guide our time together

Walking Through the Lesson:

- Describe one thing you learned from this lesson.
- What challenged you the most about this lesson?
- Discuss some ways we can build authentic fellowship and what keeps us from building authentic relationships?
- What made the fellowship in the Early Church so dynamic?
- Why is it necessary to intentionally build relationships with like-minded believers?
- How can our Christian fellowship be a witness to the world?

- Pray for one another to grow in our Christian fellowship and how that might affect the community.

Robert Rains, in his book ***New Life in the Church,*** explains:

> The church must foster and sustain the conditions in which Koinonia can be known. This cannot be done for most people simply through morning worship. Worship is indispensable as the weekly meeting of the Christian community. But it is effective only as the total sharing of all the people of the friendship in Christ they have known between Sundays.

Our Four Commitments:

- To complete the lesson for each week and be ready to share what you learned.
- To let someone in the group know if you are unable to attend the meeting.
- To pray for one another on a regular basis.
- To ask God what He is calling you to do about making disciples through building relationships, reaching out to others, and multiplying through small groups.

LESSON 5

GOD'S WORD: A LAMP FOR THE JOURNEY

Objective To know the power of God's Word working in our lives, our circumstances, and in the lives of others, and to be able to lead others to encounter the power of God's Word for themselves.

This lesson teaches us the power of God's Word to inspire us, to comfort us, and to empower us. God's Word is the vehicle through which God communicates to us. The Word is inspired and profitable for teaching, correction, and training in righteousness (2 Timothy 3:16). God's Word nourishes us and speaks to us about every area of our lives. We need His Word for the strength we receive from it, and we need God's Word to lay hold of the promises He has given to us.

Comparing *Logos* and *Rhema*

Luke describes how the witness of the disciples grew, "Then the word *(logos)* of God spread, and the number of the disciples multiplied greatly in Jerusalem" (Acts 6:7).

> *Logos*: Emphasis is on the content. *Logos* is the whole Bible. Meaning a word of explanation, divine revelation, and instruction. "Your word is a lamp to my feet and a light to my path" (Psalm 119:105). Luke continues to describe the impact of God's Word when he writes, "So the word [*logos*] of the Lord grew mightily and prevailed" (Acts 19:20).

Paul writes, "All Scripture is God-breathed and is useful for teaching, rebuking, correcting and training in righteousness, so that the servant of God may be thoroughly equipped for every good work" (2 Timothy 3:16-17, NIV).

Jesus said, "It is written, Man shall not live by bread alone, but by every word [*rhema*] that proceeds from the mouth of God" (Luke 4:4).

Jesus also said, "The words [*rhema*] that I speak to you I do not speak on My own authority: but The Father who dwells in Me does the works" (John 14:10).

The apostle Paul writes, "So then faith comes by hearing, and hearing the word [*rhema*] of God" (Romans 10:17). He also records, "The sword of the Spirit, which is the word [*rhema*] of God" (Ephesians 6:17).

Isaiah the prophet observes:

> So shall My word [*rhema*] be that goes forth from My mouth; it shall not return to Me void, but it shall accomplish what I please, and it shall prosper in the thing for which I sent it (Isaiah 55:10).

These men on the road to Emmaus were receiving the Word of God as *rhema* and their hearts burned within them. How was the Word witnessing to their spirit? Luke explains it in the verses below:

> Then their eyes were opened and they knew Him; and He vanished from their sight. And they said to one another, "did not our heart burn within us while He talked with us on the road, and while He opened the Scriptures to us" (Luke 24:31-32)?

> *Rhema* is the communication of the message. The Bible, *logos*, is the Bible in its entirety; *Rhema* is a verse from the Bible. *Rhema*: Emphasis is on the way the message is received. *Rhema* means that which is said or spoken, an utterance, in contrast to *logos*, which is the expression of a thought, a message, a discourse. *Rhema* is a spontaneous thought, idea, word, feeling, or vision.

Ephesians 6:17 says, "And take the helmet of salvation, and the sword of the Spirit, which is the word [*rhema*] of God." This refers to that portion which the believer uses as a sword in the time of need.

Mark Virkler, in his book entitled ***Communion With God*** writes, "God desires for *logos* to be translated from simple words to personal heart revelation as we pray over the Word, allowing the Spirit to cause it to live in our hearts."

What is the difference between *logos* and *rhema*?

Characteristics of God's Word:

- God's Word is **eternal**.

"The grass withers, the flower fades, but the word of God stands forever" (Isaiah 40:8). "Heaven and earth will pass away, but My word will by no means pass away" (Matthew 24:35). God's Word is an enduring word.

- God's Word is to be **in our hearts**.

"Your word I have hidden in my heart, that I might not sin against You" (Psalm 119:11). "For out of the heart the mouth speaks" (Matthew 12:34). God's Word is to be in our mouth as we speak what His is saying to us.

- God's Word **guides us** in the way we should go.

"Your word is a lamp to my feet and a light to my path" (Psalm 119:105). God's Word gives light to our lives that enables us to know His ways and His thoughts.

- God's Word **produces spiritual fruit** in our lives.

> For as the rain comes down, and the snow from heaven, and do not return there, but water the earth. And make it bring forth and bud, that it may give seed to the sower and bread to the eater, so shall My word be that goes forth from My mouth; it shall not return to Me void/empty, but it shall accomplish what I please, and it shall prosper in the thing for which I sent it (Isaiah 55:10-11).

God's Word is sown into our hearts so that it produces a life-giving word that encourages, equips, and empowers.

? Why do we need to feed on the Word of God regularly?

God's Word at Work in Us

The source of God's Word:

> Knowing this first, that no prophesy of Scripture is of any private interpretation, for prophesy never came by the will of man, but **men spoke from God as they were moved by the Holy Spirit** (2 Peter 1:20-21).

The power of God's Word:

> For the word of God is **living and powerful**, and sharper than any two-edged sword, piercing even to the division of soul and spirit, and of joints and marrow, and is a discerner of the thoughts and intents of the heart (Hebrews 4:12).

The practice of God's Word:

> Having been born again, not of corruptible seed but incorruptible, through the word of God which lives and abides forever...But the word of the Lord endures for ever...as newborn babes, **desire the pure milk of the word, that you may grow up to salvation** (1 Peter 1:23, 25, 2:2).

The purpose of God's Word:

"Your word is a **lamp** to my feet and a light to my path" (Psalm 119:105). "The entrance of Your words gives light; it gives **understanding** to the simple" (Psalm 119:130). "**Revive** me O Lord, according to Your word" (Psalm 119:107). "**Strengthen** me according to Your word" (Psalm 119:28). "For Your word has given me **life**" (Psalm 119:50). "And in His word I do **hope**" (Psalm 130:5).

> So shall My word be that goes forth from My mouth; it shall not return to Me void (without fruit), but it shall accomplish what I please, and it shall prosper in the thing for which I sent it (Isaiah 55:11).

The provision of God's Word:

God's Word provides us with wisdom in knowing His mind, purpose, and will. God's Word provides us with teaching that enriches us and strengthens us in all things that we face in life. God's Word provides words that encourage, build up, and are life-giving to others.

> Let the word of Christ dwell in you richly in all wisdom, teaching and admonishing one another in psalms and hymns and spiritual songs, singing with grace in your hearts to the Lord (Colossians 3:16).

The promise of God's Word:

> This book of the Law shall not depart from your mouth, but you shall meditate in it day and night, that you may observe to do according to all that is written in it. For then you will

> make your way **prosperous**, and then you will have **good success** (Joshua 1:8).

"Therefore whoever **hears** these sayings of Mine, and **does them**, I will liken him to a wise man who builds his house on the rock" (Matthew 7:24, emphasis added). "If you abide in My word, you are My disciples indeed. And you shall know the truth, and the truth shall make you free" (John 8:31-32).

How to Apply God's Word to Our Life

- **Prayerfully** – open the eyes of my heart (Ephesians 1:18). "And He opened their understanding, that they might comprehend the Scripture" (Luke 24:45).
- **Patiently** – "Rest in the Lord, and wait patiently for Him" (Psalm 37:7).
- **Expectantly** – "My soul, wait silently for God alone, for my expectation is from Him" (Psalm 62:5).
- **Diligently** – "Let us therefore be diligent to enter that rest" (Hebrews 4:11). Diligence means to exert oneself, make every effort, be zealous, strain every nerve. It combines thinking and acting. This word covers inception, action, and follow-through.

Another way we can refer to the Word of God:

- **Jesus is the living Word.**
  "In the beginning was the Word, and the Word was with God, and the Word was God" (John 1:1).

- **The Bible is the written Word.**
"For the word [*logos*] of God is alive and powerful" (Hebrews 4:12).
- **The Holy Spirit utters the spoken Word.**
"But the Holy Spirit teaches, comparing spiritual things with spiritual" (1 Corinthians 2:13). "It is the Spirit who gives life; the flesh profits nothing. The words [*rhema*] that I speak to you are spirit, and they are life" (John 6:63).

God's Word is good and is life giving. We open our lives to hearing Him speak to us so that we will be able to declare what He is saying to us and to others. We listen to His voice so that we may walk in obedience to Him. We hear and obey what we have heard.

Our prayer is:

Father, I want to know the power of Your Word working in my life. I ask that Your Word would go deep into my spirit and transform me in the likeness of Your Son, Jesus. Father, I submit myself to Your Word and its power to cause me to prosper in Your kingdom. Help me to grow up in the knowledge of Your Word and to release it through prayer into life's circumstances, into people's lives, and into the community. Let me experience the power of Your Word. In Jesus' name, Amen!

Group Discussion and Application

Sharing:

How did it go this week?

Opening prayer inviting the Holy Spirit to guide our time together.

Walking Through the Lesson:

- Describe one thing you learned from this lesson.
- What challenged you the most about this lesson?
- What is Logos? What is Rhema?
- How can God's word strengthen us to live an overcoming life?
- Do you have a plan on how to grow in God's word?
- What do you think it means to meditate on God's word?

- What do you think would be the benefit of meditating on His word?

John Wesley, the scholar, the author and editor of many books, was 'a man of one book'—the Bible. He accepted it implicitly and practiced it consciously. This was his secret: the Word of God.

The Bible—the Word of God—is the unveiling of Christ to the believer and to the world. It is the instructional manual for the Christian and the vehicle God uses to speak to His people. We do not worship the Bible; we worship the Author of the Bible.

—Howard Snyder
The Problem of Wine Skins

Our Four Commitments:

- To complete the lesson for each week and be ready to share what you learned.
- To attend each meeting unless there is sickness, a death or some other catastrophic event. Let someone know you will be unable to attend.
- To pray for one another on a regular basis.
- To ask God what He is calling you to do about making disciples through building relationships, reaching out to others, and multiplying through small groups.

LESSON 6

PRAYER KEEPS US ON THE JOURNEY

Objective To create an atmosphere that ushers in God's presence and makes Him welcome. We will examine important aspects of prayer, including how to model prayer and teach others how to pray. Prayer is like spiritual breathing; we inhale the life of God as we welcome Him into all areas of our lives. We exhale by surrendering ourselves to Him, only to breathe in His life once again.

This lesson focuses on learning to hear the voice God through strengthening our prayer life. Prayer is about hearing God's voice and obeying what we hear. Is that not one of the reasons why we pray—we desire to hear what God has to say about the matter? Prayer is listening for God's response to our needs, desires, opportunities or whatever the circumstance might be. Prayer is taking the time to hear the voice of God because prayer is a two-way street. God longs to speak to us.

? What does it mean to hear the voice of God?

What is Prayer?

- **Communication** - dialoguing with God.
- **Conversation** - using our natural way of speaking.
- **Coming to the Lord of all the earth**. Seek Me and I will be found by you (Jeremiah 29:13). It is the language of love. "As the deer longs for the water brooks, so longs my soul for You, O God" (Psalm 42:1).
- **Quieting the heart.** "Be still and know that I am God" (Psalm 46:10).
- **Reporting for duty.** I have come to do your will, O Lord (Hebrews 10:9).

? In what way are you learning to hear the voice of God?

Why Should We Pray?

God commands it. "And when you pray...when you pray...and when you pray...in this manner, therefore, pray" (Matthew 6:5-7, 9). We pray for His kingdom to be manifested on earth as it is in heaven. "Your Kingdom come. Your will be done on earth as it is in heaven" (Matthew 6:10).

- **It acknowledges our dependence upon Him.** "For we have no power against this great multitude that is coming against us; nor do we know what to do, but our eyes are upon You" (2 Chronicles 20:12).

- **It is the way to know His voice.** "My sheep hear My voice, and I know them, and they follow Me" (John 10:27).

? Why is it important to learn to hear God's voice?

- **It cultivates my relationship with the Lord.** "I am the vine, you are the branches. He who abides in Me, and I in him, bears much fruit; for without Me you can do nothing" (John 15:5).

- **We do not know how to pray as we ought, but the Spirit of God assists us.** "Likewise the Spirit also helps in our weaknesses. For we do not know what we should pray for as we ought, but the Spirit Himself makes intercession for us with groanings which cannot be uttered" (Romans 8:26).

How Then Shall We Pray?

- **Boldly** – "Let us therefore come boldly to the throne of grace, that we may obtain mercy and find grace to help in time of need" (Hebrews 4:16).

- **Humbly** – "God...gives grace to the humble... therefore humble yourselves under the mighty hand of God..." (1 Peter 5:5b-6a).

- **Authoritatively** – "Therefore God also has highly exalted Him and given Him the name which is above every name, that at the name of Jesus every knee should bow, of those in heaven, and of those on earth, and of those under the earth..." (Philippians 2:9-10). As the Father has taught us. "Our Father which art in heaven..." (Luke 11:1-4). A time of praise and worship: "Hallowed be Your name."

Paul exhorts us to pray "always with all prayer and supplication in the Spirit, being watchful to this end with all perseverance and supplication for all the saints" (Ephesians 6:18).

Four Truths to Increasing Our Prayer Life

A. Praying with passion:
Passionate prayer is "Deep calls unto deep" (Psalm 42:7). Out of the depths of our heart comes a yearning cry for the heart of God and for the things of God.

Praying with passion contains three elements:

- It is not passive, but proactive.
- It is not pretense, but poured out before the Lord.
- It is not placid, but diligently pursues the purposes of God.

Jeremiah writes, "Pour out your heart like water before the face of the Lord" (Lamentation 2:19). If we look in two translations, we see what the Psalmist states, "Pour out your heart **to** Him" (Psalm 62:8, NLT, emphasis added). "Pour out your hearts **before** Him; God is a refuge for us" (Psalm 62:8, emphasis added).

What do you think it means to pour out one's heart before God?

B. Praying with power is to pray in agreement.
Jesus said, "Again I say to you that if two of you agree on earth concerning anything that they ask, it will be done for them by My Father in heaven" (Matthew 18:19).

"When the Day of Pentecost had fully come, they were all with one accord in one place" (Acts 2:1). "And when they had prayed, the place where they were assembled together was shaken; and they were all filled with the Holy Spirit, and they spoke the word of God with boldness" (Acts 4:31).

Why is there power in agreement?

C. Praying with purpose:

Missionary and evangelist E. Stanley Jones describes the purpose of prayer,

> The first thing in prayer is to get God. If you get Him, everything else follows...allow God to get at you, to invade you, to take possession of you. He then pours His prayers through you. They are His prayers—God-inspired, and hence, God answered.

The purpose of prayer is to cultivate an abiding relationship with Jesus Christ. "I am the vine, you are the branches. He who abides in Me, and I in him, bears much fruit; for without Me you can do nothing" (John 15:5).

The word "agreement" means to sound together, to be in harmony, to make the same sound like a symphony.

The purpose of prayer is to advance the kingdom of God.

"And from the days of John the Baptist until now the Kingdom of heaven suffers violence, and the violent take it by force" (Matthew 11:12). "The Law and the prophets were until John. Since that time the Kingdom of God has been preached, and everyone is pressing into it" (Luke 16:16).

How is the kingdom advanced through prayer?

D. Praying with perseverance means:

- **To pray with boldness:** "Let us therefore come boldly to the throne of grace, that we may obtain mercy and grace to help in time of need" (Hebrews 4:16).
- **To pray with confidence:** "Now this is the confidence that we have in Him, that if we ask anything according to His will that He hears us" (1 John 5:14).

- **To pray with endurance:** "For you have need of endurance, so that after you have done the will of God, you may receive the promise [God's blessing upon our lives]" (Hebrews 10:36).

George Muller's nickname was "Stayer." For example,

> "The greatest point is never to give up until the answer comes. I have been praying for sixty-three years and eight months for one man's conversion. He is not saved yet, but he will be. How can it be otherwise...I am praying." The day Muller's friend received Christ did not come until Muller's casket was lowered in the ground. There near the open grave, his friend gave his heart to God. Prayers of perseverance had won another battle. Muller's success may be summarized in four powerful words: "He did not quit" (taken from ***No Easy Road***).

Bob Sorge, in his book ***In His Face,*** shares about perseverance, "God's Spirit is constantly calling us to persevere, to be steadfast, to endure patiently, to bear up and to wait."

? What do you think it means to "come boldly to the throne of grace?"

Developing a Prayer Pattern:

- A – doration
- C – onfession
- T – hanksgiving
- S – upplication

The ability to pray with power is to know that I am a child of God, that I have been birthed into the kingdom of God. I know that I am an heir of God and a joint-heir of Jesus Christ. I know that my position is not because of my goodness, but because of Christ's righteousness in me. I can pray with power not because of my name, but in the name of the One to whom I belong. I can invoke His name and know His presence, His power, His provision, His pardon, and His pleasure.

Let this be our prayer:

Lord, make me an instrument through whom Your kingdom can come and be a present reality. Teach me to pray through and not let go until the enemy is pushed back and Your purposes are established. I pray this in the strong and mighty name of Jesus.

Group Discussion and Application

Sharing:

How did it go this week?

Opening prayer inviting the Holy Spirit to guide our time together

Walking Through the Lesson:

- Describe one thing you learned from this lesson.
- What challenged you the most about this lesson?
- What does prayer mean to you? When did it become more than just a word?
- What do you think this statement means, "Prayer is the one activity that brings us into an encounter with the living God"?
- What does it mean to pray God's Word?
- How can we pray with power?
- How is prayer making a difference in you and in those around you?

It is not so much that we get prayer, but that prayer gets us. It is the language of the heart that expresses deep gratitude to the One who knows us best. Prayer is more than a function we perform as Christians. It is the positioning—the posturing—of the heart before God and reporting for duty.

Our Four Commitments:

- To complete the lesson for each week and be ready to share what you learned.
- To attend each meeting unless there is sickness, a death, or some other catastrophic event. Let someone know you will be unable to attend.
- To pray for one another on a regular basis.
- To ask God what He is calling you to do about making disciples through building relationships, reaching out to others, and multiplying through small groups.

LESSON 7

SHARING OUR FAITH ABOUT THE JOURNEY

Objective To become faith-sharing people of the Good News of Jesus Christ, to communicate the transformation He has made, and to encourage others to become faith-sharers of this Good News.

This lesson deals with our witness to the world and the impact Christ in us has to those whom God has brought into our lives. It is Christ in us that fills us with hope, not only in the life to come, but in the here and now. Because Christ has filled our hearts with His love through the Holy Spirit, we have His power at work through us demonstrating the grace and love of Christ. Because of Christ in us, we have a faith to share that is worth sharing. Christ saved us, empowered us, and equipped us to be vibrant witnesses to an unbelieving world. So, let us make an unbelieving world change their minds about Jesus.

A witness is one who shares Christ in a winsome way that glorifies God and demonstrates His love. This can be through a word, an act, or an attitude. A witness is one who makes himself available to share the goodness, grace, mercy, and love of God in word and in deed.

What do we share? (Romans 5:1-5).

- **Hope** – "Now hope does not disappoint..." (Romans 5:5). "...Which is Christ in you the hope of glory" (Colossians 1:27).
- **Faith** – "Therefore, having been justified by faith, we have peace with God through our Lord Jesus Christ" (Romans 5:1). "Faith comes by hearing and hearing the Word of Christ" (Romans 10:17).
- **Love** – "Because the love of God has been poured into our hearts by the Holy Spirit" (Romans 5:5). Love means we do not withhold the truth that will set the captive free.

Who shared their faith with you that changed your mind about Christ?

Why do we need to share our faith?

- **It is the invitation of Christ.** "You shall be My witnesses..." (Acts 1:8).
- **There is a world in need of hearing the Good News of Jesus Christ.** "Go to the highways, and as many as you can find, invite them in" (Matthew 22:9).
- **It helps us to grow as Christians.** "For to everyone who has, more will be given, he will have abundance" (Matthew 25:29).
- **We give voice to the One who called us.** Be ready to tell of the hope that is within you (1 Peter 3:15b)

How do we share our faith?

- **With meekness and reverence.** "Always be ready to give a defense to everyone who asks you a reason for the hope that is in you, with meekness and fear" (1 Peter 3:15).

How can we share Christ in a winsome way?

- **With confidence and boldness.** "And they were all filled with the Holy Spirit, and they spoke the word of God with boldness" (Acts 4:31b).
- **With humility and gratitude.** "Be clothed with humility" (1 Peter 5:5). "God gives grace to the humble" (James 4:6). "Thanks be to God for His indescribable gift" (2 Corinthians 9:15).
- **As one who is a new creation in Christ.** "Therefore, if anyone is in Christ, he is a new creation; old things have passed away; behold, all things have become new" (2 Corinthians 5:17).

Why are we able to share our new life in Christ with others?

- **As one who is daily walking in relationship to Jesus Christ.** "As you therefore have received Christ Jesus the Lord, so walk in Him, rooted and built up in Him established in the faith" (Colossians 2:6-7).

How does our daily walk with Christ affect our witness to others?

Fulfilling God's vision and becoming a faith-sharing congregation means:

- "The harvest truly is great, but the laborers are few; therefore pray to the Lord of the harvest to send out laborers into His harvest" (Luke 10:2).
- "Go therefore and make disciples...baptizing them...teaching them to observe all things that I have commanded you" (Matthew 28:19-20).
- "Go therefore and make disciples" (Matthew 28:19). "And love your God...and your neighbor as yourself" (Matthew 22:37-39).
- "So continued daily with one accord in the temple, and breaking of bread from house to house" (Acts 2:46). "...And taught publicly and from house to house" (Acts 20:20). "And with great power the apostles gave witness to the resurrection of the Lord Jesus. And great grace was upon them all" (Acts 4:33).

Sharing our faith with purpose:

- Sharing our faith helps us to fulfill our vision.
- Sharing our faith is a priority in our congregation.
- Sharing our faith is a value we hold as the community of faith in Christ.
- Sharing our faith is an intentional act we encourage all believers to be a part of, and we seek to empower others to be effectively share their faith.
- Sharing our faith is being obedient to the Great Commission and to the Great Commandment.
- Sharing our faith can be built through a network of small groups that assist us in growing and in sharing our faith.

How can we share the hope that is within us?

What do we share?

"Therefore, having been justified by faith, we have peace with God through our Lord Jesus Christ. Through whom also we have access by faith into this grace in which we stand, and rejoice in hope of the glory of God. And not only that, but we also glory in tribulations, knowing that tribulation produces perseverance. And perseverance, character; and character, hope. Now hope does not disappoint, because the love of God has been poured out in our hearts by the Holy Spirit who was given to us (Romans 5:1-5).

Why do we need to share our faith (witness)?

"Do you not say, 'There are still four months and then comes the harvest'? Behold, I say to you, lift up your eyes and look at the fields, for they are already white for harvest! And he who reaps receives wages, and gathers fruit for eternal life, that both he who sows and he who reaps may rejoice together. For in this the saying is true: 'One sows and another reaps.' I sent you to reap that for which you have not labored; others have labored, and you have entered into their labors" (John 4:35-38).

? Why do we need to be prepared to share God's love with others?

When do we share (witness)?

"But you shall receive power when the Holy Spirit has come upon you; and you shall be witnesses to Me in Jerusalem, and in all Judea and Samaria, and to the end of the earth" (Acts 1:8). "And you are witnesses of these things. Behold, I send the Promise of My Father upon you; but tarry in the city of Jerusalem until you are endued with power from on high" (Luke 24:48-49). "So Jesus said to them again, 'Peace to you! As the Father has sent Me, I also send you.' And when He had said this, He breathed on them, and said to them, 'Receive the Holy Spirit'" (John 20:21).

> ? What does the Holy Spirit give us so that we can be witnesses?

How can we share our faith (witnessing)?

"But sanctify the Lord God in your hearts, and always be ready to give a defense to everyone who asks you a reason for the hope that is in you, with meekness and fear" (1 Peter 3:15). "Therefore, if anyone is in Christ, he is a new creation; old things have passed away; behold, all things have become new" (2 Corinthians 5:17). "And when they had prayed, the place where they were assembled together was shaken; and they were all filled with the Holy Spirit, and they spoke the word of God with boldness" (Acts 4:31).

> ? What is the promise God has given to us who believe? When Jesus breathed upon His disciples whom did He say to receive according to John 20:22-23?

Glenn McDonald, in his book ***The Disciple Making Church,*** observes, "A disciple is a follower, a learner of Jesus Christ. A disciple of Jesus means intentionally presenting ourselves to Christ every day so that our thoughts, words, actions, and motives might become more like His."

A witness is one who shares Christ in a winsome way that glorifies God and demonstrates His love through a word or act. A witness is one who makes himself available to share the goodness, grace, mercy, and love of God in word and deed.

Let this be our prayer:

Lord, make me a witness to the transforming power of Jesus Christ. Make me a powerful witness that transcends fear, timidity, and reluctance. Lord, Jesus, I offer myself to You to be Your instrument of love and grace to others. I make myself available to You and to Your Spirit to be a witness to the life, death, and resurrection of Jesus Christ. Amen!

Group Discussion and Application

Sharing:

How did it go this week?

Opening prayer inviting the Holy Spirit to guide our time together

Walking Through the Lesson:

- Describe one thing you learned from this lesson.
- What challenged you the most about this lesson?
- What is your greatest fear about witnessing?
- Who witnessed to you? Who told you about their faith and caused you to begin to have your own experience with Christ?
- When have you shared your faith with someone else?
- Are there individuals you can begin praying for that they would come to know Jesus for themselves?

- Why do we need the Spirit's power to witness?

- Pray for one another to be filled with the Holy Spirit and to be a powerful witness to Jesus Christ.

A witness is not what I do; it is who I am, because of the personal transformation of Christ in my life—I am a witness!

Our Four Commitments:

- To complete the lesson for each week and be ready to share what you learned.
- To attend each meeting unless there is sickness, a death, or some other catastrophic event. Let someone know you will be unable to attend.
- To pray for one another on a regular basis.
- To ask God what He is calling you to do about making disciples through building relationships, reaching out to others, and multiplying through small groups.

LESSON 8

THE FAITH THAT ACTS ON THE JOURNEY

Objective To declare that God is the God of increase, and that He wants us to increase in knowing Him and growing in His grace. God wants us to have an ever increasing faith—the kind of faith that moves mountains, the kind of faith that believes that with Him nothing is impossible, and the kind of faith that expects great things from God, and for Him to do great exploits through us.

God is the God of Increase

The apostle Paul writes, "I planted, Apollos watered, but God gave the increase, so then neither he who plants, nor he who waters, but God who gives the increase" (1 Corinthians 3:6-7). The Psalmist writes "May the Lord give you increase more and more...and increase in the knowledge of God... and grow with the increase that is from God" (Psalm 115:14-15; Colossians 1:10, 2:19).

The word "increase" means: to super-abound, have in excess, excel. The word shows the generosity of God's grace giving assurance that faithful use of one's talents and gifts sets the stage for one's own advancement.

God wants us to increase in four areas:

1. **First of all, God wants us to increase in wisdom.** Luke 2:52 says, "Jesus increased in wisdom." If Jesus, the Son of God increased in wisdom, then we too must increase in wisdom. Wisdom is God's spoken word to us as we learn to hear His voice. Being filled with the fullness of the Spirit: "that you may be filled with the knowledge of His will in all wisdom and spiritual understanding" (Colossians 1:9).

2. **Second, God wants us to increase in faith.** Luke 17:5 "And the apostle said to the Lord, 'Increase our faith.'" We must see that God is ever increasing in us as Abraham did, "He did not waver at the promise of God through unbelief, but was strengthened in faith, giving glory to God" (Romans 4:20).

    - **By exercising our faith.** "For to everyone who has, more will be given, and he will have abundance..." (Matthew 25:29).

    - **By listening for God's voice.** "So then faith comes by hearing, and hearing by the Word of God" (Romans 10:17).

3. **Third, God wants us to increase in strength.** Isaiah 40:29 reads, "He gives power to the weak, and to those who have no might He increases strength."

God wants to increase our strength:

- It is God's purpose to take us from "strength to strength" (Psalm 84:7).
- It is through God's power working in us. "Strengthened with all might through His Spirit in our inner man" (Ephesians 3:16; Colossians 1:11).
- It is through God's provision "I can do all things through Christ who strengthens me" (Philippians 4:13).

4 **Fourth, God wants us to increase.** "Then the Word of God spread, and the number of the disciples multiplied [increased] greatly…" (Acts 6:7). We have to see that God is ever increasing in us. If we are not increasing, we are decreasing; we cannot stay the same. God is not the God of lack, but the God of increase. God is the not the God of shortage, but the God of more than enough. God is not the God of limitations, but the God for whom nothing is impossible. God is not the God of frugality, but the God of generosity.

God is the one who supplies all things. Paul wrote, "Now may He who supplies seed to the sower, and bread for food, **supply** and multiply the seed you have sown and **increase** the fruits of your righteousness (2 Corinthians 9:10, emphasis added).

> The word "supply" means generously, what is needed, to supply fully or abundantly. God supplies an abundance of grace. "Therefore He who supplies the Spirit to you and works miracles among you." (Galatians 3:5).

God wants His church to increase:

- **In reaching entire households.** "And believers were increasingly added to the Lord, multitudes of both men and women" (Acts 5:14).
- **In salvations.** "And the Lord added [increase] to the church daily those who were being saved" (Acts 2:47).
- **In growing disciples.** "So the churches were strengthened in the faith, and increased in number daily" (Acts 16:5).
- **In fruitfulness.** "That you may walk worthy of the Lord, being fruitful in every good work and increasing in the knowledge of God" (Colossians 1:10).

We are God's workmanship, and His work in us is a supernatural work of His grace. God's grace is at work in us and through us. "For we are God's fellow workers. You are God's field; you are God's building. According to the grace of God which was given to me, as a wise master builder I have laid the foundation..." (1 Corinthians 3:9-10)

We are God's workmanship because God's grace **enables** our hearts to receive all He has for us, **helps** us to welcome His presence into our midst, **stirs** up a great hunger for His working in our lives, **creates** an atmosphere for His building to take place, and **captures** our hearts to desire what He is doing.

Paul uses a building to communicate God is working on us. "You are God's building" (1 Corinthians 3:9). We need to build a structure that welcomes His presence and carries His anointing (power).

> Having been built on the foundation of the apostles and prophets, Jesus Christ Himself being the chief cornerstone, in whom the whole building, being fitted together, grows into a holy temple in the Lord, in whom you also are being built together for a dwelling place of God in the Spirit (Ephesians 2:20-22).

Peter declared whom the foundation would be built upon as he responds, "You are the Christ, the Son of the Living God" (Matthew 16:18).

- God was the **source** of Abraham's faith; he was looking for "the city which has foundations, whose builder and maker is God" (Hebrews 11:10).
- God is the **standard** by which we measure all things. "Go through, go through the gates! Prepare the way for the people; build up, build up the highway! Take out the stones, lift up a banner for the peoples!" (Isaiah 62:10).

A banner signifies: victor, overcoming, more than a conqueror. This is the banner we stand under. Jesus, our victorious One who conquered death, the grave, and everything humanity can do to Him, arose victorious, and we stand under that same banner today: victorious, overcoming, and more than a conqueror. *God of grace and God of glory visit us in this hour and pour out your Holy Spirit upon us until our hearts are met with yours.*

Jesus is Our Foundation

Jesus is our foundation. "For no other foundation can anyone lay than that which is laid, which is Jesus Christ" (1 Corinthians 3:11). Jesus said, "I am the way, the truth and the life, no man comes to the Father but through me" (John 14:6). Peter states, "There is salvation in no one else! There is on other name in all of heaven for people to call on to save them" (Acts 4:12, NLT); His name is Jesus. The heart of the gospel is Jesus Christ:

> In the beginning was the Word, the Word was with God, and the Word was God. He was in the beginning with God...In Him was life, and the life was the light of men...And the Word became flesh and dwelt among us, and we beheld His glory, the glory as of the only begotten of the Father, full of grace and truth" (John 1:1-2, 4, 14).

Isaiah declares, "Behold, I lay in Zion a stone for a foundation, a tried stone, a precious cornerstone, a sure foundation" (28:16).

? What does it mean to make Jesus the foundation of our faith?

Jesus is the foundation upon whom we stand and build our lives.

- Has the ability to impart (to fill us up) with the abundant life of God.
- Has the capacity to empower (to give us authority) to live an overcoming life.
- Has the substance (the stuff) to do the works He did.

Jesus Christ is the central figure of the gospel. "For there is one God and one Mediator between God and men, the Man Christ Jesus" (1 Timothy 2:5). Jesus is the foundation upon whom we build our lives. Jesus left us four things that He did: to preach the Good News, to heal the sick, to deliver those held captive by the enemy, and to make disciples. Therefore, if our life is built upon Him, then we must do the things He did.

Jesus is the foundation upon which we build our lives and upon which the church is built.

> "And I also say to you that you are Peter, and on this rock I will build my church, and the gates of hell shall not prevail against it. And I will give you the **keys** of the kingdom of heaven, and whatever you **bind** on earth will be bound in heaven and whatever you **loose** on earth will be loosed in heaven" (Matthew 16:18-19, emphasis added).

To "bind" means to tie up, to no longer be able to harm, to take power from, and to leave them ineffective—

> forbidding. If someone is bound by sin, the church can share the freedom we have in Christ. "Just as Christ was raised from the dead by the glory of the Father, even so we also should walk in newness of life" (Romans 6:4).

Peter is the not the rock Jesus is talking about because Jesus uses the word "*petra*," which is a foundation rock or boulder to speak of Himself. The word Jesus used for Peter is the word "*petros*," a fragment of the "*petra*." Peter describes it this way, "You also, as living stones [*petroi*], are being built up a spiritual house" (1 Peter 2:5). We are all living stones, but Jesus is the Rock.

These verses detail our confession:

- Our confession flows from the heart and is **declared** by our lips.
- Our confession **demonstrates** we have an abiding relationship to Jesus Christ.
- Our confession is the **diligence** we show in holding fast to the One who holds all of our promises.

We discover these truths about why Jesus is our foundation:

A. This is an unveiling of the heart by God to see who Jesus really is. "For flesh and blood has not revealed this to you, but my Father who is in heaven" (Matthew 16:17). It is God's download from His heart to ours about His Son, Jesus. The truth of the power of Jesus Christ penetrates the heart and mind to understand and to grasp the truth about Jesus: who He is, what He has done, what He will do, and be for us. Where the love of God overwhelms the heart and we become sons and daughters, filled with the Spirit of the living God.

B. This becomes our personal confession about Jesus Christ: "You are the Christ, the Son of the living God" (Matthew 16:16). Our confession comes from our lips, "For with the heart one believes...and with the mouth confession is made..." (Romans 10:10) John, in his epistle, writes, "Whoever confesses that Jesus is the Son of God, God abides in him, and he in God" (1 John 4:15). The writer of Hebrews exhorts, "Let us hold fast the confession of our hope without wavering, for He who promised is faithful" (Hebrews 10:23).

C. Jesus has given us His authority to carry on His ministry. "And I will give you the keys of the kingdom of heaven" (Matthew 16:19a) Jesus said to those who helped remove the stone from where Lazarus lay, "Loose him and let him go" (John 11:44). "Keys" denote authority: Jesus has passed the mandate on to us to continue His work until He returns.

Jesus has given us His authority to:

- Be vessels of healing and release (removing stones that bind).
- Be instruments of announcing good news to those who have been held captive all their lives.
- Be voices declaring the Good News of Jesus that it is He who sets us free.

Jesus said to the woman who had a spirit of infirmity for eighteen years and was bent double and could not stand upright "Woman, you are loosed from your infirmity" (Luke 13:12).

> To "loose" means to let go, to untie, to set free—no longer permitting the enemy to cause destruction, chaos, and disorder in one's life.

The Lord said, "Just as the Son of Man did not come to be served, but to serve and to give his life a ransom for many" (Matthew 20:28). The word "ransom" means to loose; it signifies a release from slavery or captivity. It defines the price paid cancelling our debt. Jesus bound sin to Himself in order to loose us from its power, bondage, and control. "Therefore if the Son makes you free, you shall be free indeed" (John 8:36).

Our Prayer is:

Lord, Jesus, You are the foundation upon whom I build my life, the One upon whom I can trust implicitly. Jesus, You are the person to whom I place my trust and faith that enables me to remain unshaken when everything around me is in chaos. Lord, Jesus, I find in You the source of peace, the song of joy in my heart, and the One who declares Himself as faithful and true. Lord, Jesus, I surrender all of me to all of You.

Group Discussion and Application

Sharing:

How did it go this week?

Opening prayer inviting the Holy Spirit to guide our time together

Walking Through the Lesson:

- Describe one thing you learned from this lesson.
- What challenged you the most about this lesson?
- What are we to increase in and what causes increase to happen in our lives?
- How and in what way can we increase in the things of the Spirit?
- What are we doing when we build our lives upon Jesus Christ?
- What does it mean that Jesus is the foundation of our faith?

- What does it mean that we are God's workmanship?

- What does it mean that God has given to us the keys of the kingdom?

- What does it mean to bind and loose?

Our Four Commitments:

- To complete the lesson for each week and be ready to share what you learned.
- To attend each meeting unless there is sickness, a death, or some other catastrophic event. Let someone know you will be unable to attend.
- To pray for one another on a regular basis.
- To ask God what He is calling you to do about making disciples through building relationships, reaching out to others, and multiplying through small groups.

BIBLIOGRAPHY FOR SECTION ONE

Chambers, Oswald, ***My Upmost For His Highest***. New York: Dodd, Mead and Company, 1935.

Clark, Randy, ***Power, Holiness and Evangelism***. Shippensburg, PA: Destiny Image Publishers, 1999.

Crabb, Larry, ***Finding God***. Grand Rapids, MI: Zondervan Publishing, 1995.

Ellis Joe, ***The Church on Purpose***. Cincinnati, OH: Standard Publishing, 1982.

Helland, Roger, ***The Journey Walking with God***. Tonbridge Kent, England: Sovereign World Ltd, 2000.

McDonald, Glenn, ***The Disciple Making Church***. Grand Haven, MI: Faith Walk Publishing, 2004.

Eastman, Dick, ***No Easy Road***. Grand Rapids, MI: Baker Book House, 1971.

Piper, John, ***A Hunger For God***, Wheaton, IL: Crossway Books,, 1997.

Rains, Robert, ***New Life in The Church***. New York: Joanna Cotler Books, 1961.

Sorge, Bob, ***In His Face***. Canandaigua, NY: Oasis House Publishing, 1994.

Synder, Howard, ***The Problem of Wine Skins***. Dowers Grove, IL: Inter Varsity Press, 1975.

Virgo, Terry, ***Restoration in the Church***. Columbia, MO: Cityhill Publishing, 1989.

Virkler, Mark, ***Communion With God***. Shippensburg, PA: Destiny Image Publishers, 1990.

Section Two

JOURNEY IN DISCIPLESHIP

Growing in Christ-Likeness

INTRODUCTION

Learning to Stand Fast

Paul writes to the Philippian church and encourages them to "stand fast in the Lord" (4:1). The phrase "stand fast" is actually one word in the Greek and means to persevere. It means to remain in the "faith" as they professed Jesus Christ as Lord. Paul is saying: don't move away from that foundation. The earliest declaration we have of the early church is "Jesus Christ is Lord," and it is in Him that we stand strong in the faith.

We must recognize our weakness to stand faithfully, steadfastly, and unwaveringly. The Bible says, "Let the weak say I am strong" (Joel 3:10). Isaiah observes, "He gives power to the weak, and to those who have no might he increases strength" (40:29). Paul writes, "For my strength is made perfect in weakness" (2 Corinthians 12:9b).

The word "perfect" means to bring to maturity. 2 Corinthians 12:9 could read: my faith is matured when I acknowledge my weakness and declare my strength is in the Lord. To recognize our weakness is to humble ourselves under the mighty hand of God (1 Peter 5:6). Paul warns us about living independently and in self-confidence: "Let him who thinks he stands take heed lest he fall" (1 Corinthians 10:12). Paul learned the secret of living the abiding life in Christ: "My gracious favor is all you need. My power works best in weakness." So now I am glad to boast about my weaknesses, so that the power of Christ can work through me" (2 Corinthians 12:9, NLT). As a new creation, we live from the power of God—His divine nature living in us—as we surrender to His Lordship in our lives.

We can stand fast in the faith through the finished work of Christ. Paul encourages the church at Thessalonica, "For now we live, if you stand fast in the Lord" (1 Thessalonians 3:8). As a new creation in Christ we cannot add to what He has done for us on the cross and in the resurrection. He has given us His Spirit as a down payment that we belong to Him. This is the abundant life Jesus promised.

What does it mean to rest in the finished work of Christ?

- We can **add nothing** to what Christ has done for us. "I have **finished** the work which You have given Me to do" (John 17:4, emphasis added).

- We have been **forgiven** past, present, and future. "In Him we have redemption through His blood, the forgiveness of sins, according to the riches of His grace" (Ephesians 1:7). Through the shedding of Christ's blood we were redeemed (past tense); He paid the price for us through the shedding of His blood.

- We have a new found **freedom** in Christ. "Stand fast [steadfast, unwavering, faithful] therefore in the freedom by which Christ has made us free, and do not be entangled again with a yoke of bondage" (Galatians 5:1).

Peter Bellini, professor at United Theological Seminary observes, "At the cross, Jesus took the sins of the world unto himself and destroyed the power of sin and the devil. Because I trust in Christ, sin and death have no power over me."

We can stand fast in the faith in the midst of adversity. If there is adversity then there must be an adversary. Peter, in his epistle, explains, "Be sober, be vigilant [watchful]; because your adversary the devil walks about like a roaring lion, seeking whom he may devour. Resist him, steadfast in the faith" (1 Peter 5:8-9).

As a new creation in Christ we are to stand fast against our adversary and to remain strong in the Lord, "Therefore take up the whole armor of God, that you may be able to withstand in the evil day, and having done all, to stand" (Ephesians 6:13). The idea is the ability to stand our ground against the evil one who comes only to steal, kill, and to destroy and following the battle we are still standing.

As a new creation we can grow in Christ-likeness:

- As we keep our eyes on Jesus who has delivered us from the power of darkness and transferred us into the kingdom of the Son of His love (Colossians 1:13).
- As we guard our heart above all else, for it determines the course of our life (Proverbs 4:23, NLT).
- As we know that nothing will separate us from the love of God who makes us more than conquerors through Him who loved us (Romans 8:37, 39).

Let this be our prayer:

Father, we come to You in all of our brokenness, weaknesses, faults, and failures looking to You to strengthen us in our inner man to stand firm in the faith. Father, strengthen us to rest in the finished work of Jesus and strengthen us to be victorious over our adversary that comes only to steal, kill, and destroy what You have done for us and in us. Amen!

LESSON 1

GROWING IN CHRIST-LIKENESS

Let's examine four values that enable us to grow spiritually and in Christ-likeness.

First of all, choose to move beyond drinking milk to eating solid food. "Therefore, laying aside all malice, all deceit, hypocrisy, envy and all evil speaking, as newborn babes, desire the pure milk of the Word, that you may grow up to salvation" (1 Peter 2:1-2).

George Barna defines "discipleship" as, "Becoming a complete and competent follower of Jesus Christ. It is about intentional training of people who voluntarily submit to the Lordship of Christ and who want to become imitators of Him in every thought, word and deed."

There is a basic desire for having more of the Lord and for the Lord to have more of us. The word "desire" means "to long for" or "to crave." The spiritual milk referred to is referenced in 1 Peter 1:25: "For the Word of the Lord endures forever." Jesus said, "Man shall not live by bread alone, but by every Word that proceeds out of the mouth of God" (Matthew 4:4).

> The Word of the Lord endures, and "we live by every Word that proceeds from the mouth of God." The word used here is *rhema* meaning a now-word. It identifies with us; it bears witness with our spirit; it speaks to us right now. It brings peace, joy, assurance, promise, and confidence.

? Why is it important to feed upon God's Word regularly?

Facts about spiritual maturity:

- It is not automatic—problems do not disappear, but Christ in us makes us more than conquerors.
- It is a process—becoming like Christ is something that will continue throughout our lifetime.
- It takes discipline to grow—God's unmerited favor (grace) enables us to enjoy the journey.

- It takes resting in God—this is the place of revelation (insight and understanding). "Let us therefore be diligent to enter that rest" (Hebrews 4:11). The word "diligent" means to exert oneself, making every effort and straining every nerve. It covers inception, action, and follow-through. Jesus is coming back for a mature bride without spot or wrinkle.

Second, spiritual growth becomes a priority in our lives (1 Peter 2:3). "Now that you have tasted that the Lord is good." We find in 2 Peter 3:18, "But grow in the grace and knowledge of our Lord and Savior Jesus Christ" (NIV). The verb "grow" is the same verb John the Baptist used when he said, "He [Christ] must increase [grow], but I must decrease" (John 3:30). It means we come into the fullness of who we are in Christ. We understand it is Christ in us, the hope of glory. The word "decrease" does not mean belittlement, depreciation, or condemnation, but a clear statement that Christ desires to be all in all.

According to 2 Peter 3:18 what two things are we to grow in? Why?

Spiritual growth therefore requires:

- A hunger and desire for more of the Lord.
- Let us "lay aside every weight, and the sin which so easily ensnares us, and let us run with endurance the race that is set before us" (Hebrews 12:1).
- That we be child-like in receiving the things of the kingdom of God.

When Jesus called men and women to follow Him, making disciples was a priority in His life as found in Luke 6:12-13 which says, "Now it came to pass in those days that He went out to the mountain to pray, and continued all night in prayer to God. And when it was day, He called His disciples to Himself; and from them He chose twelve." He did not call the most successful or the most talented, but He did call those who were willing to devote their lives in following Him.

George Barna, in his book ***Growing True Disciple***s, observes from his research, "Three of every five adults we surveyed told us they want to have a deeper commitment to the Christian faith, but they are not involved in any intentional effort to grow spiritually."

Third, spiritual growth means we are discovering our place of significance in Christ and in His church.

> Coming to Him as to a living Stone, rejected indeed by men, but chosen by God and precious, you also, as living stones, are being built up a spiritual house, a holy priesthood, to

offer up spiritual sacrifices acceptable to God through Jesus Christ (1 Peter 2:4-5).

- Discovering our place of significance is found in "coming to Him as to a Living Stone."
- We are being built together for a habitation of the presence of God. "In whom the whole building, being fitted together, grows into a holy temple in the Lord, in whom you also are being built together for a dwelling place of God in the Spirit" (Ephesians 2:21-22).
- Our calling is to be, "a holy priesthood." We can come into the presence of Christ anytime, anywhere, and any place.

? According to 1 Peter 2:4-5 what are we called to be and what does that mean?

Paul Cedar writes, "The key to a good self-image is found in the image of what we are in Jesus Christ. It is His image that is available to us as we trust in Christ Jesus."

Our identity is not in **doing**, but in our **being** what Christ has called us—"living stones."

> ? Why do you think it is important to find our significance in Christ?

Lastly, spiritual growth is learning to make all of life a worship experience. We were created for worship—"to offer up spiritual sacrifices acceptable to God through Jesus Christ" (1 Peter 2:5). "But you are a chosen generation, a royal priesthood, a holy nation, His own special people, that you may proclaim the praises of Him who called you out of darkness into His marvelous light" (1 Peter 2:9).

- **Sacrifice is not a sacrifice until it is given away.** What then is the sacrifice? "Therefore by Him let us continually offer the sacrifice of praise to God, that is, the fruit of our lips, giving thanks to His name" (Hebrews 13:15).

- **When we discover that all of life is worship, we can sing:** "I worship you almighty God, there is none like you..." David exclaimed, "Therefore you are great, O Lord God, for there is none like you" (2 Samuel 7:22). Hannah's prayer for a child was answered and she declared, "No one is holy like the Lord, for there is none besides you, nor is there any rock like our God" (1 Samuel 2:2). We can praise God all day long for there is none like Him in all the earth.

- **When we discover that all of life is worship, we can offer ourselves fully to Christ:** "We bring the sacrifice of praise into the house of the Lord and we offer up to you a sacrifice of thanksgiving and we offer up to you a sacrifice of praise."

  Paul states, "I beseech you therefore, brethren, by the mercies of God, that you present your bodies a living sacrifice, holy, acceptable to God, which is your reasonable service" (Romans 12:1).

- **When we discover that all of life is worship, we can declare:** "Bless the Lord, Oh my soul and all that it is within me, bless His holy name." According to Psalm 103, we are not to forget all His benefits, "He forgives us...He heals us...He redeems us...He crowns us with loving-kindness and tender mercies...He satisfies our mouth with good things...He renews our youth like the eagles."

  When we begin to make all of life a worship experience, our prayer is, "Open the eyes of my heart Lord, open the eyes of my heart—I want to see Jesus; I want to see Him."

> Which one of the above five ways of making all of life a worship experience spoke to you? Why?

God puts a testimony in our hearts, and we speak of it with our lips. As the Psalmist states, "Let my mouth be **filled** with your praise and with your glory all the day" (71:8).

> The word "filled" means filling something up to the brim. May we be filled and overflowing with praise to God.

> What one thing are you asking God to do during our time together?

To grow spiritually is not optional. We purposely position our hearts to receive more of the Lord, poised to give ourselves more fully to Him and to grow into His likeness to become fully devoted followers of Jesus Christ.

Group Discussion and Application

Sharing:

How did it go this week? (A time of informal sharing)

Opening prayer inviting the Holy Spirit to guide your time together

Walking Through the Lesson:

- Take time to review the lesson for this week and go over any questions that the group members might have.
- What challenged you the most about this lesson?
- Why must spiritual growth become a priority?
- Why do we need to move from milk to eating solid food (spiritually speaking)?
- How and in what ways can we make all of life a worship experience?
- Why do you think discovering and knowing who we are in Christ is so important?

- According to 1 Peter 2:9, who does God say we are? How does this impact our view of ourselves and of God?

- What does it mean to you to grow spiritually?

- What are you asking God to do in your life in light of this lesson?

Our Four Commitments:

- To complete the lesson for each week and be ready to share what you learned.
- To let someone in the group know if you are unable to attend the meeting.
- To pray for one another on a regular basis.
- To ask God what He is calling you to do about making disciples through building relationships, reaching out to others, and multiplying through small groups.

LESSON 2

RADICAL OBEDIENCE

In Luke chapter 5, we find in this story four fishermen who have been fishing all night and have come up empty. The next day as they were cleaning their nets to go back out fishing, Jesus asked to use one of the boats from which He would preach. Because the people were crowding Jesus so much, He was about to be backed into the lake, and He needed more room. These fishermen were glad to lend Him their boat while He spoke to the people on the bank.

When Jesus finished His message, He spoke to the fisherman to "launch out into the deep and let down your nets for a catch" (Luke 5:4). This was no small request because it meant getting their boats ready to go out fishing once again with no promise of a great catch. What made this request so appealing? Were they touched by the message Jesus had been proclaiming? Was it something deep within them that caused them to simply obey the words of Jesus? We will call it radical obedience.

Mark Rutland, in his book ***Launch Out Into the Deep*** states, "Wherever we are spiritually, God's call is for us to move onward. Choose your own metaphor—higher ground, a closer walk, another step—it is the call of God by the Holy Spirit to greater growth and maturity through obedience and faith. The command to launch out into the deep is simply the insistence of the Lord that we go on with Him."

? What did **radical obedience** mean to Peter and his fishing partners?

A. First of all, it was a complete trust in His Word. "Master, we have toiled all night and caught nothing; nevertheless at your Word I will let down the net" (Luke 5:5). Peter and his friends did not have a history with Jesus. He was a stranger to them, but something rose up within them and said, "What do we have to lose, let's try it or at least let's just agree to do this." This would be radical obedience—taking Jesus at His word and watching to see what would happen.

Radical obedience is called agreement: agreeing with God as to what He wants to do. It is the opposite of resistance.

Peter and his fishing buddies did not add any qualifying statements to what Jesus was asking such as, "Let's go tonight when we do most of our work" or "We would be glad for you to ride along with us." Radical obedience is doing what God asks of us—coming into agreement with what He is asking and trusting Him for the outcome. God's grace will enable us to trust Him completely!

The invitation of Christ demands:

- A response to **obedience.** "Nevertheless at your word."
- A demonstration of **faith**. "I will let down the net."
- A **teachable** spirit. "Teach me your way, O Lord; I will walk in your truth" (Psalm 86:11).

Dick Wills, in his book ***Waking to God's Dream,*** observes:

> It is that obedience that God honors and blesses. This means a daily walk with God that more and more leads me to live a surrendered life. I have to give up trying to control the ministries of the church. I have to give up my thinking the way I would like the church to be. I have to give up everything except a tenacious desire to do the will of God.

Why do you think radical obedience is important in following Christ?

B. Second, radical obedience is launching out into the deep at the invitation of Christ. "'Launch out into the deep and let down your nets for a catch.' [Peter] answered...'Master, we have toiled all night and caught nothing; nevertheless at Your word I will let down the net'" (Luke 5:4-5).

Why is the call of Christ always invitational?

The point of this story is that what we could not do on our own, the unmerited favor of God (grace) does for us. "And when they had done this, they caught a great number of fish, and their net was breaking" (Luke 5:6).

What did Peter and his friends do to receive this blessing of an overwhelming catch of fish? Nothing. They just put their nets in the water, and the fish came to their nets, jumping to get in. The fish wanted to have bragging rights as having been part of a miracle.

God wants us to grow to the point that we trust Him and that we experience His amazing grace—His unmerited favor. God wants us to succeed and to experience the abundance of His blessings. This begins to happen as we cooperate/agree with what He wants to do. Peter and his friends cooperated, agreed with what Jesus wanted to do, and they got blessed as a result. "So they signaled to their partners in the other boat to come and help them, and they came and filled both the boats, so that they began to sink" (Luke 5:7).

C. Third, radical obedience is launching out into the deep and discovering there is yet more of Christ to experience. As Peter encountered the power of God he fell down on his knees and said,

> "Depart from me, for I am a sinful man, O Lord!" For he and all who were with him were astonished at the catch of fish which they had taken. Jesus said to Simon, "Don't be afraid from now on you will be catching men (Luke 5:8, 10).

? What difference did this event make in the life of Peter and his friends?

Radical obedience is a desire to know Jesus, to follow Him, and to experience the riches of His presence, "So when they had brought their boats to land, they forsook all and followed Him" (Luke 5:11).

For Peter and his fishing friends it meant:

- Trusting Jesus and His life giving words.
- Experiencing the extravagance of God's grace.
- Encountering Jesus is a life-changing event.

D. Finally, radical obedience is launching out into the deep and discovering a fuller, deeper, and richer relationship with Jesus Christ. Jesus said, "Do not be afraid. From now on you will catch men" (Luke 5:10). As a result of this astounding experience of the "more" of Christ, "They forsook all and followed Him" (Luke 5:11).

God wants to make it clear: He wants us to be successful. He will bring to you whatever you need to accomplish His plan, purpose, and mission.

To experience God's power:

- Is to **realize** how much He loves us.
- Is to **recognize** our dependence upon Him.
- Is to **receive** His grace—His unmerited favor—toward us.
- Is to **rest** in the fact that God wants us to succeed and to bless us abundantly.

We cannot live on what was, our previous experience, or our comfort zone. The beck and call of God insists that we come and follow Him. We enter into a "new, life-giving way that Christ has opened up for us...by means of His death" (Hebrews 10:20).

Radical obedience of launching out into the deep means:

- "By faith Abraham **obeyed** when he was called to go out to the place which he would receive...and he went out, not knowing where he was going" (Hebrews 11:8, emphasis added).

- "By faith Noah, being divinely warned of things not yet seen, moved with godly fear, **prepared an ark**" (Hebrews 11:7, emphasis added). God said to Noah, launch out and build a boat and I will bring the water to you.

- "By faith they [people of Israel] **passed through** the Red Sea as by dry land, whereas the Egyptians, attempting to do so, were drowned" (Hebrews 11:29, emphasis added).

How then do we experience the "more" of God?

- By saying "yes" to the Lord and all that He has for us.
- By saying "yes" to the Lord's invitation to be a part of what He is blessing.
- Peter and his friends could add nothing to what had just happened; they simply said "yes" to what Jesus wanted to do.

? What would it mean to you to experience the "more" of God?

Record your prayer for this lesson:

Group Discussion and Application

Sharing:

How did it go this week? (A time of informal sharing)

Opening prayer inviting the Holy Spirit to guide your time together

Walking Through the Lesson:

- Take time to review the lesson for this week and go over any questions that the group members might have.
- What spoke to you the most about the need for radical obedience?
- How do you think Peter was feeling when Jesus asked him to launch out into the deep?
- What did Mark Rutland's statement mean to you?
- What did Dick Wills' statement say to you about the church?

- Describe what Christ's invitation to radical obedience says to you.

- What do you think we discover about Christ when we launch out into the deep?

- What do you think it means to experience the "more" of God?

- What are you asking God to do in your life in light of this lesson?

Our Four Commitments:

- To complete the lesson for each week and be ready to share what you learned.
- To let someone in the group know if you are unable to attend the meeting.
- To pray for one another on a regular basis.
- To ask God what He is calling you to do about making disciples through building relationships, reaching out to others, and multiplying through small groups.

LESSON 3

AN OVERCOMING LIFE

John, in his epistle, asks this rhetorical question about the overcoming life: "Who is he who overcomes the world, but he who believes that Jesus is the Son of God" (1 John 5:5). Having Jesus Christ in our lives makes us an overcomer, not because of what we have done, but what Jesus has done for us on the cross. Jesus never intended for us to live a defeated life; He declared, "I have come that you might have life and life abundantly" (John 10:10). Jesus meant for this to be a present reality.

> The word "overcome" means conquer, triumph over, prevail over, and rise above. God has enabled us to do this through His unmerited favor called grace.

If we are to look at anyone in Scripture who lived an overcoming life it would be Jesus. "...But was in all points tempted as we are, yet without sin" (Hebrews 4:15b). Paul writes, "For He made Him who knew no sin to be sin for us, that we might become the righteousness of God in Him" (2 Corinthians 5:21).

This was the greatest exchange that ever happened on the face of the earth: **our sinfulness for God's righteousness**. John, in his epistle, writes, "Because as He is, so are we in this world" (1 John 4:17). We are aware of the three temptations Jesus faced in the wilderness, and yet, there is something more we can discover about how Jesus lived an overcoming life.

A. First of all, Jesus lived an overcoming life because He submitted to the Spirit's leadership in His life. "Then Jesus, being filled with the Holy Spirit, returned from the Jordan and was led by the Spirit into the wilderness" (Luke 4:1). Jesus was both filled and led by the Spirit.

When we submit to the Spirit's leadership:

- We gain **insights** we may not have had before to realize there is a spiritual battle going on, and we must do spiritual warfare.

- We can **occupy** the place we are in because God fills us with wisdom to deal with everything we might face.

- We are **cooperating** with the Spirit's purpose for our lives. That is, we are not resisting the Spirit's work in us, but resting in the Spirit's work in us.

In your own words explain why it is important to submit (surrender, yield, accept) to the Spirit's leadership in our lives.

B. Second, Jesus lived an overcoming life because He understood clearly who He was. His Father declared, "You are my beloved Son; in you I am well pleased" (Luke 3:22). Jesus did not have an identity crisis. He knew who He was and lived from the position of Son-ship. Jesus did not seek the approval of man because He stood approved before His heavenly Father. In two of the three temptations of Jesus, the devil sought to cause Him to question His identity by saying, "If you are the Son of God..." (Luke 4:3, 9).

Jesus kept His eyes upon His heavenly Father and that resulted in an overcoming life. Understanding who we are in Christ will cause us to know that we are God's beloved sons and daughters in whom He is well pleased (Romans 8:15-16). "We are a royal priesthood...We are God's own special people...We have been called out of darkness into His marvelous light" (1 Peter 2:9) to enjoy unbroken fellowship with Christ.

> ? Why does the devil, the enemy, attack us at our identity in Christ? Why do you think it is important to know who we are in Christ?

C. Third, Jesus lived an overcoming life because He had us in mind. "Now thanks be to God who always leads us in triumph in Christ, and through us manifests the fragrance of His knowledge in every place" (2 Corinthians 2:14). Jesus said, "In the world you will have tribulation, but be of good cheer, I have overcome the world" (John 16:33). Paul writes, "But thanks be to God, who gives us the victory through our Lord Jesus Christ" (1 Corinthians 15:57).

Jesus knew if the devil could cause Him to question His identity it would rob Him of His destiny, His purpose and His mission. We, too, will need to know our identity in Christ so that our destiny, purpose, and mission are fulfilled.

D. Finally, Jesus overcame because the wilderness experience would catapult (launch, send forth) Him into ministry and His future. "Then Jesus returned in the power of the Spirit to Galilee, and news of Him went out through all the surrounding region" (Luke 4:14). This experience would take Jesus to a new level of living, a greater sense of His purpose and mission. The evidence of living an overcoming life is that we are submitted to the Spirit's work in our lives. When we understand that we are in Christ, what we go through takes us to greater fruitfulness in Christ and living the grace-filled life.

Paul writes, "That you may **walk** worthy of the Lord, fully pleasing Him, being fruitful in every good work and increasing in the knowledge of God" (Colossians 1:10, emphasis added). John, in his epistle, writes, "For whatever is born of God overcomes the world. And this is the victory that has overcome the world—our faith" (1 John 5:4).

> The word "walk" in the New Testament always conveys a person's lifestyle, that is, how they live their life before an unbelieving world.

Jesus said, "In the world you will have tribulation; but be of good cheer, I have overcome the world" (John 16:33). Since Jesus overcame and He is living in us, then the only conclusion we can draw is that He makes us overcomers. We find in Job the necessary things to know about living as overcomers in this world:

> But He knows the way that I take; when he has tested me, I shall come forth as gold. My foot has held fast to His steps; I have kept His ways and not turned aside. I have not departed from the commandment of His lips; I have treasured the words of His mouth more than my necessary food (Job 23:10-12).

According to this passage from Job how can we live an overcoming life?

Job gives us several insights to an overcoming life:

- Know that God is weaving something precious, valuable, and eternal into the fabric of our lives.
- Know that God gives us grace to stand in the midst of adversity.
- Know that God is increasing the measure of our faith through obedience.
- Know that God's Word is the treasure that sustains us.

> So He humbled you, allowed you to hunger, and fed you with manna which you did not know nor did your fathers know, that He might make you know that man shall not live by bread alone; but man lives by every Word that proceeds from the mouth of the Lord (Deuteronomy 8:3).

From the four mentioned insights above, which one spoke to you the most and why?

Listed below are five ways we can live an overcoming life:

- We walk by **faith**, fully trusting the Lord. "We walk by faith, not by sight" (2 Corinthians 5:7).
- We walk in the **Spirit**, engaging in fellowship with Him. "Let us walk in the Spirit..." (Galatians 5:16).
- We walk in **love** because God is love. "And walk in love, as Christ also loved us..." (Ephesians 5:2).
- We walk as children of **light**, because He called us out of darkness into His marvelous light (1 Peter 2:9). "For you were once darkness, but now you are light in the Lord. Walk as children of light" (Ephesians 5:8).
- We walk just as **Jesus** walked because He lives in us. "He who abides in Him ought himself also walk just as He walked" (1 John 2:6). "As you therefore have received Christ Jesus the Lord, so walk in Him" (Colossians 2:6).

Why do you think our walk of faith is related to how we live an overcoming life?

Record your prayer for this lesson:

Group Discussion and Application

Sharing:

How did it go this week? (A time of informal sharing)

Opening prayer inviting the Holy Spirit to guide your time together

Walking Through the Lesson:

- Take time to review the lesson for this week and go over any questions that the group members might have.
- What spoke to you the most about living the overcoming life?
- What was your greatest discovery from this lesson?
- Describe in your own words what you believe the overcoming life is.
- How can Jesus' example of the wilderness experience be an encouragement to us?

- What do you think holds us back from living the overcoming life?

- How does our faith help us in living an overcoming life?

- What does this statement mean to you, "If it matters to you, it matters to God"?

- How or in what ways are you going to apply this lesson to your life?

Our Four Commitments:

- To complete the lesson for each week and be ready to share what you learned.
- To let someone in the group know if you are unable to attend the meeting.
- To pray for one another on a regular basis.
- To ask God what He is calling you to do about making disciples through building relationships, reaching out to others, and multiplying through small groups.

LESSON 4

THE WHOLENESS THAT ONLY CHRIST CAN GIVE

Paul writes, "Now may the God of peace Himself sanctify [set you apart] completely; and may your whole spirit, soul and body be preserved blameless at the coming of our Lord Jesus Christ" (1 Thessalonians 5:23). Paul's prayer is that we experience the peace of God, be set apart for His use, and that He would bring wholeness (completeness, fullness) to our lives.

The word "peace" means a state of rest, quietness, and the absence of strife. The word carries the inner peace we experience with God and the outer peace we enjoy with others. The way to peace is not looking inside, but looking outside to Jesus, the Author and Finisher of our faith (Hebrews 12:2).

The peace of Christ sustains us in the midst of chaos, conflict, and uncertainty. Jesus is the source of our peace:

a sense of rest, calm, and assurance. The peace this world offers is fleeting, temporary, and superficial. Jesus is our peace because He resides in us and does an internal work in us that expresses itself outwardly. We have peace with God because we can cast all our cares upon Him.

Let's look briefly at three individuals who needed to experience God's wholeness in their lives. Jesus is identified as the Prince of Peace (Isaiah 9:6) and it is He who has given His life so that the separation between man and God would be united through the peace of Christ "having made peace through the blood of the cross" (Colossians 1:20). Jesus came to give us His peace: "Peace I leave with you, My peace I give to you; not as the world gives do I give to you. Let not your heart be troubled, neither let it be afraid" (John 14:27).

A. First, in Mark 5:1-20 we find a man living in the tombs totally out of control and isolated from the rest of the world. Jesus, the Prince of Peace, does a mighty work in this man. "Then they [the townspeople] came to Jesus, and saw the one who had been demon possessed and had the legion, **sitting** and **clothed** in his **right mind**...Jesus said, 'Go home to your friends, and tell them what great things the Lord has done for you, and how He has had compassion on you" (Mark 5:15, 19, emphasis added).

This man experienced the wholeness that only Christ can give:

- **Sitting** – It is the posture of receiving all that Jesus has to give. Paul writes that Christ "raised us up together, and made us sit together in the heavenly places in Christ Jesus" (Ephesians 2:6).

- **Clothed** – It is the position of dignity, restoration, and healing. Isaiah declares, "I will greatly rejoice in the Lord, my soul shall be joyful in my God; for He has clothed me with the garments of salvation, He has covered me with the robe of righteousness" (Isaiah 61:10).

- In his **right mind** – It is the possessing of right believing that produces right doing. "He began to proclaim in Decapolis all that Jesus had done for him; and all marveled" (Mark 5:20). From our fragmented lives Jesus fills our steps with purpose and mission.

? Which of the above manifestations (sitting, clothed, in his right mind) spoke to you the most? Why?

B. The **second** person we want to look at is the man who needed another touch of Jesus upon his life as recorded in (Mark 8:22-26). In this lesson, we will address our need for spiritual vision. Whether that means renewed vision or a new vision, it is all about getting God's vision for ourselves and for what He is doing. In this verse, we find that Jesus has entered the town of Bethsaida and was mobbed by a crowd asking Him to touch their friend so that he might receive his sight. Jesus is moved to action by the prayers of His people. We find again and again those who brought their friends and relatives to Jesus needing His touch upon their lives and how Jesus was moved by compassion to address those who were in need. How many of us have cried out for new vision and have allowed the Lord to lead us from old, familiar places? Sometimes our familiar surroundings tend to blind us to what God desires to do.

There are three observations we can make about Jesus restoring this man's vision:

- **The blind man realized he needed someone to lead him.** "So He took the blind man by the hand and led him" (Mark 8:23). Isaiah speaks of those needing spiritual vision, "I will bring the blind by a way they did not know; I will lead them in paths they have not known…I will make darkness light before them" (Isaiah 42:16). Jeremiah observes, "O Lord, I know the way of man is not in himself; it is not in man who walks to direct his own steps" (Jeremiah 10:23).

- **The blind man could only go where Jesus took him as He** "… led him out of town" (Mark 8:23). This speaks of our dependence upon the Lord. It requires that we trust Him and demands our surrendering to His leading. For Jesus to do the deeper work in this man's life, He took him out of the familiar to another place "out of town." What did they talk about on their journey out of town? What questions did Jesus ask this man? Did the man ever ask Jesus, "Where are we going? Where are you taking me?"

- **The blind man was willing to do whatever it took to receive his sight, even if it meant a second touch.** "And when He had spit on his eyes and put His hands on him He asked if he saw anything... Then He put His hand on his eyes again and made him look up, and he was restored and saw everyone clearly" (Mark 8:23, 25). Spitting represents Jesus' own life, His DNA, which was the source of the man's healing and wholeness. Jesus wants us to experience His very life and His touch upon our lives. There is a necessity in our obedience to do what we don't understand. We conclude that God's ways are higher than our ways, and His thoughts are higher than our thoughts (Isaiah 55:8). God desires to restore our spiritual vision and to bring wholeness and healing to our lives. He delights in taking us by the hand and leading us to where we cannot go on our own.

Jesus led the blind man out of town to heal him. The first time He touched his eyes vision came, but the man's spiritual vision was not clear. What do I mean by "spiritual" vision? It is to look at things from God's perspective, asking Him to open the eyes of our hearts. It means to look at things through the Holy Spirit, not the natural mind. **The key to God's ability to lead us is in the realization we need to be led.** God will deliver us from the familiar and the comfortable, and He will take us to a new place in Him where we have not been before because He loves us too much to leave us as we are.

> Why do you think it is important for us to come to the realization we need Jesus to lead us?

C. The **third** person we want to look at is the woman caught in adultery who needed to receive from Jesus the gift of no condemnation and wholeness to her fragmented life (John 8:1-12). This story is not so much about what Jesus actually writes in the sand or why the man did not stand with her to be stoned. This story is not so much about sin finding you out, or who will throw the first stone. These are not the main points of the story. The story is about the gift of no condemnation. When we believe and place trust in Christ alone for our salvation, we become "in Christ." We are brought into His family to abide with Him forever.

The gift of no condemnation brings wholeness to our lives because God's Word is:

- **Life-giving.** "The Words that I speak to you are spirit, and they are life" (John 6:63). This woman stands for all who are in need of hearing the life-giving Words of Jesus, "Neither do I condemn you."

The word "life" is not mere existence, but fullness in our spirit, soul, and body. The word "condemnation" means rebuke, accuse, and to find guilty. Paul writes, "Therefore there is **now** no condemnation for those who are in Christ Jesus" (Romans 8:1, emphasis added). The word "now" is very important. It does not mean after we die, but "now"—this very moment—we stand free from all condemnation because Jesus took our condemnation (rebuke, guilt, and shame) upon Himself.

- **Liberating.** "And you shall know the truth and the truth shall make you free...Whom the Son sets free is free indeed" (John 8:32, 36). God's Word tells us who we are in Christ and what He has done for us through Christ. This woman stands for all who are in need of experiencing Christ's freedom from the tormenting thoughts, shame, and guilt that only He can bring because He carried it away on the cross.

- **Light.** "I am the light of the world. He who follows me shall not walk in darkness, but have the light of life" (John 8:12). Jesus exposes the darkness and the lies of the enemy that produce only guilt, condemnation, and defeat. This woman stands for all who are in need of God's light to get rid of all darkness, all defeat, and all lies that the enemy uses to hold men captive all the days of their lives. We know that we can walk in the light because Jesus is in the light, and we can enjoy an unbroken fellowship with Him.

- **Healing.** "Then your light shall break forth like the morning, your healing shall spring forth speedily, and your righteousness shall go before you; the glory of the Lord shall be your rear guard" (Isaiah 58:8). The word "healing" means restoration of life, deliverance, and refreshing. This woman stands for all who are in need of God's healing touch upon their lives bringing wholeness, completeness, and release from those things that have held them captive all the days of their lives. Jesus looked tenderly at this woman and asked her, "'Woman, where are those accusers of yours? Has no one condemned you?' She said, 'No one, Lord.' And Jesus said to her, 'Neither do I condemn you; go and sin no more'" (John 8:10-11). Jesus did not come to condemn us, but to save us, to deliver us, to heal us and to make us whole.

? Which one of these four things are you needing God's Word to do in your life?

Record your prayer for this lesson:

Group Discussion and Application

Sharing:

How did it go this week? (A time of informal sharing)

Opening prayer inviting the Holy Spirit to guide your time together

Walking Through the Lesson:

- Take time to review the lesson for this week and go over any questions that the group members might have.
- What spoke to you the most about the wholeness that only Christ can give?
- What do you think was the greatest need for the demoniac as described in Mark 5:1-20?
- How would you describe the transformation that took place in the demonized man?
- Why do you think we need a second, third and additional touch of God upon our lives?

- How liberating do you think the words of Jesus were to the woman caught in adultery, "Neither do I condemn you; go and sin no more" (John 8:11)?

- What does this mean to us: "There is now no condemnation for those who are in Christ Jesus?"

- How or in what ways are you going to apply this lesson to your life?

Our Four Commitments:

- To complete the lesson for each week and be ready to share what you learned.
- To let someone in the group know if you are unable to attend the meeting.
- To pray for one another on a regular basis.
- To ask God what He is calling you to do about making disciples through building relationships, reaching out to others, and multiplying through small groups.

LESSON 5

RELENTLESS FAITH

We find that relentless love has its reward because faith works by love. Chuck Pierce observes, "Love is the only way we will come into a new dimension of faith. When we break into faith, we will break into miracles. We must create a faith atmosphere that is greater than the atmosphere we have been in up to this point."

We find in Mark 1:45 that the presence of Jesus drew a crowd: "And they came to Him from every direction." The crowd followed Jesus into the house where He liked to stay in Capernaum; some believe it was Peter's house. As we find, "Immediately many gathered together, so that there was no room" (Mark 2:2). It was a packed house. We find a similar situation in Mark 7:24, "And he entered a house and wanted no one to know it" Jesus arrived at the home hoping to remain anonymous, but was unable to do so, "But He could not be hidden" (Mark 7:24). The NLT states it, "He tried to keep it a secret that He was there, but He couldn't. As usual, the news of His arrival spread fast." Here is the truth: Jesus can't be hidden.

> Jesus was not into building programs, technology, media, or megachurches. He was about the business of empowering people to seek the lost, strengthen the weak, heal the sick, bind up the injured, and bring back those who had strayed. Not a program, but a radical demonstration of the power of God.
>
> —Michael Slaughter, ***Unlearning Church***

We can make two observations concerning making room for God:

1. **First** of all, making room for God means we invite Him into our house (our lives, our hearts). "And they came to Him from every direction...and it was heard that He was in the **house**" (Mark 1:45-2:1, emphasis added).

The word for "house" is *okios* meaning our home, family, the workplace, network of friends, and congregation. There is not an area of our lives into which we can't invite Jesus and welcome His presence.

2. **Secondly,** making room for God means we make room for His Word. "And He preached the word to them" (Mark 2:2). Let His seed take root in your lives. "Now the seed is the Word of God" (Luke 8:11). "Let the Word of Christ dwell in you richly" (Colossians 3:16).

When you hear the phrase "making room for God," what does that mean to you?

Four men could not get their friend into the presence of Jesus one way so they began to make another way—they made room, space, an opening through which Jesus had opportunity to touch their friend's life significantly. James in his epistle explains, "Draw near to God and He will draw near to you" (James 4:8).

These four men made room for Jesus to work on their friend's behalf:

A. First of all, making room for God means that we learn to press through.

> Soon the house where He was staying was so packed with visitors that there wasn't room for one more person, not even outside the door. And He preached the word to them (Mark 2:2, NLT).

This is the pivotal point in the story that Mark is describing—if they allowed discouragement to overcome them, they would have walked away. If they became disillusioned, they would have become critical and cynical. Yet, they refused to become discouraged or cynical. They chose to press through all the objections, obstacles, and distractions because they would not be denied the opportunity to bring their friend to Christ. They were willing to do whatever it took. Jesus said, "The Law and the prophets were until John. Since that time the kingdom of God has been preached, and everyone is pressing into it" (Luke 16:16).

These four men, carrying their paralytic friend, could have said, "There is no way to get to Jesus. The house is too crowded." Or they could have said, "We'll come back later," but by that time Jesus could have moved on to another place. The question was: how badly did they want it? Were they willing to make the sacrifices needed to find a way? Would they walk away thinking what could have been?

B. Secondly, making room for God means we seek to find a place of entrance into His presence. "They couldn't get to Jesus through the crowd, so they dug through the clay roof above His head..." (Mark 2:4, NLT). "Go through, go through the gates [doors, place of entrance]! Prepare the way for the people...Take out the stones, lift up a banner for the peoples!" (Isaiah 62:10). These men went to another level of prayer and intercession for their friend. They said, "We'll tear the roof off the house, and we will create a gate or window—a 'portal' as an entrance to the presence of Christ." They were creating a place for God to use. They were removing obstacles that might keep them from His presence, "So when they had broken through" (Mark 2:4). Mark declares, not "if" they could break through, but "when" they broke through.

C. Finally, making room for God means refusing to deviate from the purpose God has put into your heart. "Then they lowered the sick man on his mat, right down in front of Jesus. Seeing their faith, Jesus said to the paralyzed man" (Mark 2:4b-5, NLT).

They could have formed a committee or a task force to study the situation and examine all their options. Then they could have voted on which one to go with and still be left standing holding their paralyzed friend with his unmet need. When there is a sense of mission and purpose, urgency and action are required. There are times when the clock of eternity is ticking away and our opportunities become smaller and smaller. If not now, when?

Let's make some observations about what these men did for their friend:

- They were on a mission.
- Their steps were filled with purpose.
- They knew now was the time to act.
- There was a sense of urgency in their pursuit of God's presence. When it seems as if there is no room, breakthrough is just around the corner.

When it seems that there is no room, will we press through into the presence of Christ at all cost? When it seems that there is no room, will we determine to seek Christ's presence and bring our need before Him? When it seems that there is no room, will we refuse to deviate from the mission and purpose God has put within our hearts? So what is it that creates that place of entrance—

the place that brings us into the presence of God? It is our faith—faith working through love.

What happened as these men activated their faith?

- They **relentlessly** pressed through the obstacles that stood between them and Jesus—between their barrier and their miracle.
- Their **radical** faith did not go unnoticed. Jesus saw their faith.
- The **reassuring** words of Jesus gave them hope as they heard Jesus speaking words of healing and restoration to their friend.
- They **raised** their voice in praise to God as they "were amazed and glorified God, saying, 'We never saw anything like this'" (Mark 2: 12).

The church was never the same after that day as they witnessed this miracle, "The man jumped up, took the mat, and pushed his way through the stunned onlookers" (Mark 2:12, NLT). Terry Teykl, in his book ***The Presence-based Church*,** describes it this way, "The presence of God overflowed onto unsuspecting worshipers that day. Like holy lava cascading down the sides of a volcano, the essence of God's holiness, power, love and grace were evident to all in the house."

? What is standing between you and the miracle you need?

Record your prayer for this lesson:

Group Discussion and Application

Sharing:

How did it go this week? (A time of informal sharing)

Opening prayer inviting the Holy Spirit to guide your time together

Walking Through the Lesson:

- Take time to review the lesson for this week and go over any questions that the group members might have.
- Describe one thing you learned from this lesson.
- What were the three elements about Jesus' call to discipleship according to Mark 3:14-15? What does this say to us about discipleship?
- What kind of things do we have to press through in order to make room for God?
- How or in what way can we make entrance places into the presence of Christ?

- We looked at the four things that happened when these four men activated their faith. Which one spoke to you and why?

- What does this phrase mean to you, "When they had broken through?" What is the picture that these words paint?

- Why do you think Jesus forgave this man's sins before healing his body?

- How or in what ways are you going to apply this lesson to your life?

Our Four Commitments:

- To complete the lesson for each week and be ready to share what you learned.
- To let someone in the group know if you are unable to attend the meeting.
- To pray for one another on a regular basis.
- To ask God what He is calling you to do about making disciples through building relationships, reaching out to others, and multiplying through small groups.

LESSON 6

ABIDING FAITH

We found in the lesson last week that four men let their friend down through the roof of the house because they desperately wanted to get him in the presence of Jesus. People will go where His presence is because in His presence is fullness of joy and life forever more (Psalm 16:11). Now that Jesus is in the house we must learn to host His presence. Paul writes, "Do you not know that you are the temple of the Holy Spirit?" (1 Corinthians 6:19). Peter describes that we are "living stones being built to be a spiritual house" (1 Peter 2:5).

The Shunammite woman is a wonderful example of how we can make room for God as we learn to host His presence (2 Kings 4:8-10). The Lord asked the Prophet Isaiah, "Heaven is My throne, and earth is My footstool. Where is the **house** that you will build Me? And where is the place of My rest?" (Isaiah 66:1, emphasis added). We are the house of the Lord, and His desire is that we welcome Him so that from this earthen vessel flows the life and presence of the living God.

God is looking for individuals and congregations who will make room for God. God is looking for those who have the heart of this Shunammite woman who will welcome Him, make room for Him, entertain His presence, and provide a place of habitation for Him.

The truth is we can occupy a place in God and never experience the depth of His mercy and grace. Sometimes we hold the Lord at bay and are never really able to embrace His mercy and grace, the outpouring of love, and the affection He has for us.

We see three things this Shunammite woman was willing to do in hosting the presence of God:

A. First of all, she was willing to clear things out of the way in order to make room for the Lord. She said, "Please, let us make..." a place where he does not just visit, but to provide a place of **habitation** (2 Kings 4:10) She said, "Look now, I know that this is a holy man of God who passes by us regularly" (v. 9). Let's move from God just passing by to creating a place for Him to take up residence in you—a place of **transformation**. Elisha asked her, "What can I do for you?" (v.13).

This woman got hold of the present move of God as seen and personified through the prophet Elisha. This is the sequence of events as she moved from providing a place of:

- Visitation to
- Habitation to
- Transformation

This woman was singled out because she made room for God. These are some of the attributes she possessed:

- She was notable – she was a person of affluence.
- She was persuasive – she often asked the prophet Elisha to come and to eat with her and her husband.
- She was hospitable – what was hers she shared with him.
- She was wise – she drew near to the prophet Elisha because Elisha personified the present move of God at that time. She was wise enough to pick up on the present move of God and find a way to entertain the presence of God. She literally made her house irresistible to God. She provided such a warm reception that he could not pass by without stopping in for a meal and fellowship.

What do you think it means to clear the way in order to make room for God? How are we learning to host His presence?

B. Secondly, she was willing to rearrange some things in order to make room—to provide place for the Lord. "Let us make a small upper room and put a bed in it and a table and chairs and a lamp; so that whenever he comes to us, he can turn in there" (2 Kings 4:10). They had to rearrange their lifestyles, their schedules, and their priorities to make room for the Lord. We give the Lord what we have, and we ask Him to fill it with Himself: "For the earth will be filled with the knowledge of the glory of the Lord, as the waters cover the sea" (Habakkuk 2:14). God will fill whatever you bring before Him. The only limitation is what we bring to Him to fill.

She was willing to reorganize her home and to experience some inconvenience to accommodate and to host the present move of God as seen through the prophet Elisha. We must do likewise if we are to embrace the present move of God today.

She wanted to know God more and in essence was saying, "Let's expand and make room for more of God than what we are presently experiencing." Isaiah encouraged the people of God, "Enlarge the place of your tent, and let them stretch out the curtains of your dwellings; do not spare; lengthen the cords, and strengthen your stakes" (Isaiah 54:2).

She wanted the presence of God in her house all the time, and she made room for Him. "Do you not know that your body is the temple of the Holy Spirit who is in you, whom you have from God, and you are not your own" (1 Corinthians 6:19)?

This is what resulted as she rearranged her life to make room for God:

- It became a priority.
- She did whatever it took to enlarge the place for the Lord to dwell.
- She removed the limited borders of her dwelling to make room for the unlimited power of God.

How and in what ways are we making room for God in our lives?

C. Finally, in order to make room for God we must have the heart of John the Baptist like the Shunammite woman. "I must decrease and He must increase" (John 3:30). We will need to learn to remove the limitations we put on the Lord. His disciples made room for Jesus; after fishing all night, He told them, "Throw your net on the right side of the boat, and you'll get plenty of fish" (John 21:6, NLT).

The presence of God:

- Will become a **priority** for us, "But **one thing** is needed, and Mary has chosen that good part, which will not be taken away from her" (Luke 10:42, emphasis added)

- Will become the **desire** of our heart: "One thing I have desired of the Lord, that will I seek; that I may dwell in the house of the Lord all the days of my life, to behold the beauty [delightfulness] of the Lord" (Psalm 27:4).

- Will become the place of **strength and blessing** in us: "The Lord will give strength to His people; The Lord will bless His people with peace" (Psalm 29:11).

- Will become the place of **refreshing and renewing** that flows through us: "He who believes in Me, as the Scripture has said, out of his heart will flow rivers of living water. But this He spoke concerning the Spirit, whom those believing in Him would receive..." (John 7:38-39).

If we want God's presence to dwell with us, then we will need to make room, expand, reorganize, and begin doing whatever it takes to accommodate Him, to host Him, and to entertain His presence. It means we will need to become more flexible. As someone rightly said, "Blessed are the flexible. When they bend they will not break." Making room for God means we need to make room to hear His voice—for Him to speak to us. This becomes a priority before advancing forward.

The secret to God's presence is *waiting*. Waiting means resting. Resting means trusting:

- **Wait** upon the Lord. "Wait on the Lord; be of good courage, and He shall strengthen your heart; wait, I say, on the Lord" (Psalm 27:14).

- Those who wait upon the Lord will be **empowered** to do what He calls them to do. "But those who wait on the Lord shall renew their strength" (Isaiah 40:31).
- Waiting upon the Lord results in the **joy** of the Lord. "Behold this is our God; we have waited for Him…we will be glad and rejoice in His salvation" (Isaiah 25:9).

Waiting is not a bad thing. Waiting is one of the most powerful things we can do because we are acknowledging our heavenly Father as our Source, and we will not go forward until we have heard from Him.

Record your prayer for this lesson:

Group Discussion and Application

Sharing:

How did it go this week? (A time of informal sharing)

Opening prayer inviting the Holy Spirit to guide your time together

Walking Through the Lesson:

- Take time to review the lesson for this week and go over any questions that the group members might have.
- Describe one thing you learned from this lesson.
- What spoke to you the most about making room for God in this lesson?
- What is the purpose of making room for God? Why must it become a priority?
- Why is God looking for more than just a visitation, but a place where He can inhabit?

- What does it mean that our body is the temple of the Holy Spirit?

- What would it look like to reorder our lives to make room for God?

- What does it mean to wait upon the Lord?

- How or in what ways are you going to apply this lesson to your life?

Our Four Commitments:

- To complete the lesson for each week and be ready to share what you learned.
- To let someone in the group know if you are unable to attend the meeting.
- To pray for one another on a regular basis.
- To ask God what He is calling you to do about making disciples through building relationships, reaching out to others, and multiplying through small groups.

LESSON 7

SUPERNATURAL FAITH

We found in Mark's account of the paralyzed man lowered down by his friends into the presence of Jesus that he discovered forgiveness and healing while Jesus was in the house. Next, we discovered we must learn to host the presence of God as the Shunammite woman did by adding on a room to her house just to accommodate God's presence and by welcoming Him into every area of her life. Now we will examine what God asks us to do once He is in the house (in our hearts and lives). Our example is the woman fixing the last meal for herself and her sons in 2 Kings 4:1-7 and how God wonderfully provided for her every need and added years to her life and the lives of her sons.

When we don't keep up to date with our relationship to Christ:

- We become spiritually dull; we can't discern between good and evil.

- We just don't have the spiritual power in our lives to resist evil.
- We become lethargic in our prayer life as someone said, "The first thing to go when we become spiritually dull is our prayer life."

A. First of all, the prophet Elisha asked her, "What do you have?" You start with what you have and then see what God will do with it. The woman replied, "Your maidservant has nothing in the house but a jar of oil" (2 Kings 4:2). She thought she needed more in order to move the hand of God. You may have just a little bit of faith—it may be the size of a mustard seed (Matthew 17:20), but just give Jesus what you have. In the New Testament, the little boy said, I only have five loaves and two fish (John 6:9). But I'll give you what I have. Here, the prophet wanted to show this woman that God takes our lack—our shortage—and creates abundance. The servants at the wedding said, "They have no wine."...Jesus said to them, "Fill the waterpots with water" (John 2:3, 7), and they filled them with water. Jesus turned the water into wine. In making room for God, we begin by allowing Him to give us a new perspective or a new view of looking at things. Our eyes do not need to focus on what we don't have because **our lack becomes God's opportunity**.

God is not so concerned about what you do not have, but that you give Him what you do have; He will supply the rest. She came to a place where her present experience with God was not enough and could not hold what God was getting ready to do. God takes what we have and uses it.

Why do you think Elisha asked the woman, "What do you have?"

B. Secondly, making room for God means we obey what He asks us to do. Even if it seems foolish—do it anyway! "Go, borrow vessels [jars] from everywhere, do not gather just a few" (2 Kings 4:3). The Lord was saying, "Give me something to fill—let me demonstrate My glory." We find in the book of Judges that God will bring his people to "a place where there is no lack of anything that is on the earth" (Judges 18:10). God says, "Give Me your past, and I will remove your shame. Give Me your present, and I will put something in your hand. Give Me your future, and I will fill it with hope and promise." As the psalmist declares, "And blessed be His glorious name forever! And let the whole earth be filled with His glory" (Psalm 72:19).

Here's the progression:

- She came to a place of brokenness—of humility.
- She declared her need.
- The Lord gave her instructions to follow.
- She obeyed with passion and commitment.
- She gave the Lord what she had, and He took it and added to it and even multiplied it.

What was the purpose of gathering as many empty jars as she could?

Paul writes to the church at Ephesus, "To know the love of Christ which passes knowledge; that you may be filled with all the fullness of God" (3:19). The word "fullness" points to a broad-based spirituality, balanced through participating in all of God's blessings, resources, and wisdom. It is the recognition of truth by personal experience. This widow collected all she could in her desperation to be obedient to the Lord. Her prayer might have been, "Lord lead me to lots of jars, put jars in my hand, give me favor in gathering jars that You may fill and display Your glory.

C. Thirdly, God is going to work from the inside out. "And when you have come in, you shall shut the door behind you and your sons; then pour it [a jar of oil] into all those vessels, and set aside the full ones" (2 Kings 4: 4).

God begins in our hearts. He lets us see the change He is making. He lets us experience what only He can do. He allows us to participate in His miracle working power. He allows us to see the display of His glory, and it becomes our testimony of God's grace and activity in our lives. "So she went from him and shut the door behind her and her sons, who brought the vessels to her; and she poured it out" (2 Kings 4:5).

He asks us to bring empty vessels so that He might fill them with Himself—with purpose and with meaning. God changes us from the inside out as we cooperate with God's plan. This woman made room for a climate (atmospheric, environment, condition) change to take place in the room (in her heart) where she was. The climate changed from fear to faith, from despair to hope, from discouragement to encouragement, and from death to life.

This is what God was doing on the inside of this woman as she gathered jars of oil for God to fill:

- God says, "I want to release something through you that will stir up your faith."
- God says, "I want to release something through you that will raise your expectations."
- God says, "I want to release something through you that will create hope."
- God says, "I want to release something through you that will create an opportunity."

> ? Why do you think it was necessary for God to begin the change in her heart before things began to change on the outside, considering the circumstances where she was?

D. Finally, God fills vessels like no one else can. "When the vessels were full...Go, sell the oil and pay your debts; and you and your sons live on the rest" (2 Kings 4:6-7). The miracle took place on the inside and manifested on the outside. The preparation was done in the secret place. The provision and promise of God took place as she poured out what she had and then invested what she had to the glory of God. God caused the increase. God filled these vessels for His use and for His glory.

The key to this miracle was that she began to, "Seek first the kingdom of God and His righteousness, and all these things shall be added to you" (Matthew 6:33). The Bible speaks of what God did in the early church, "And the Lord added to the church daily those who were being saved" (Acts 2:47). The Lord will add and even multiply what we have for the display of His glory. As this woman collected empty jars to add to what she already had, God filled them, adding years, purpose, and meaning to her life.

We find these particular truths:

- God wants to add something to your life that you may not be presently experiencing.
- God wants to add something to your life that will express His nature and character.
- God wants to add something to your life that will make a difference in someone else's life.
- God wants to add something to your life that will add value to the kingdom of God on earth as it is in heaven.

The woman made room for God to move in a wonderful way as she:

- Acknowledged her need.
- Invited God into the midst of her need.
- Allowed Him to do the inner work that only He can do.
- Witnessed with her sons the miracle of God filling empty vessels.
- Declared the truth that Paul would later record, "And My God shall supply all your needs according to His riches in glory by Christ Jesus" (Philippians 4:19).

> ? Could we become one of those places where people come and leave filled with God's hope, love and grace? Could we be a people through whom the power of a transformed life can be seen as it begins on the inside and demonstrates itself outwardly?

Record your prayer for this lesson:

Group Discussion and Application

Sharing:

How did it go this week? (A time of informal sharing)

Opening prayer inviting the Holy Spirit to guide your time together

Walking Through the Lesson:

- Take time to review the lesson for this week and go over any questions that the group members might have.
- Describe one thing you learned from this lesson.
- What spoke to you the most about making room for God?
- What was the predicament this lady was in? What was the purpose in the woman gathering empty jars?
- According to Ephesians 3:19, who are we to be filled with? What do you think it means to be filled with the fullness of God?

- How does God take our brokenness and bring forth fruitfulness and blessing?

- Of the four things that God adds to our lives which one spoke to you the most and why?

- How or in what ways are you going to apply this lesson to your life?

Our Four Commitments:

- To complete the lesson for each week and be ready to share what you learned.
- To let someone in the group know if you are unable to attend the meeting.
- To pray for one another on a regular basis.
- To ask God what He is calling you to do about making disciples through building relationships, reaching out to others, and multiplying through small groups.

LESSON 8

ACTIVATING YOUR FAITH

We first looked at Mark's account of the paralyzed man who was lowered down by his friends into the presence of Jesus and who discovered forgiveness and healing while Jesus was in the house. Next, we discovered we must learn to host the presence of God as we saw in the Shunammite woman adding on a room to her house just to accommodate God's presence and welcoming Him into every area of her life. We looked at what God asks us to do once He is in the house (in our hearts and lives) as we saw with the woman who was fixing the last meal for herself and her sons. We saw how God wonderfully provided for her every need and added years to her life and the lives of her sons. We now want to turn our attention to making room for God when it is our choice.

The choice is how much room we will make available for Him. Will we give him enough room to give us partial victory or room enough that we can enjoy full victory? We have gone from inviting Jesus into the house (our lives) to learning to host His presence, to adding things to our lives that feed us, nourish us and give us a hope and a future. Now we will discover how we can be strategic in how we will live our lives before the Lord and before others, becoming fully devoted followers of Jesus and ultimately disciple-makers.

Joash, King of Israel was asked to do a simple thing. It might have seemed to be a bit odd or strange, but it was God's Word to him through the prophet Elisha. The act was to shoot an arrow out the window. This is learning to live our lives from the inside out because change always begins in the heart and manifests itself outwardly (2 Kings 13:14-19).

Making room for God means we believe He is going to pass on something of Himself to us. Elisha said to Joash, "'Put your hand on the bow.' So he put his hand on it, and Elisha [personification of God's presence] put his hands on the King's hands" (2 Kings 13:16). The Hebrew language conveys the idea that Elisha stood behind the king and put his arms around him in order to put his hands on the king's hands. King Joash was cloaked in the hand and voice of Elisha.

God looks for a people whom He can embrace and clothe with His power, His grace, and His love. It is God's desire to pass or to impart something of Himself to us and through us.

The Bible mentions other times when God's hands were extended through others. For example when Moses died, Joshua took his place, "Now Joshua the son of Nun was full of the Spirit of wisdom, for Moses had **laid his hands** on him" (Deuteronomy 34:9, emphasis added).

Paul wrote to Timothy to remind him of what God imparted to him, "Do not neglect the gift that is in you, which was given to you by prophesy with the **laying on of the hands** of the eldership" (1 Timothy 4:14, emphasis added).

Jesus speaks of the ministry of the Holy Spirit, "Behold, I send the Promise of My Father upon you; but tarry in Jerusalem until you are **endued [clothed or cloaked]** with power from on high" (Luke 24:49, emphasis added). We must have the power of God working on our behalf to live overcoming lives in this life and to have an impact that touches the lives of others now and for eternity.

We can make these observations from the above statements:

- God **imparts** something of Himself that expresses His character and nature.
- God **surrounds** and encompasses us with His love.
- God **demonstrates** through us His power and might.
- God **stirs** up His gifts within us.

> ? What do you think it means that God wants to pass on something of Himself to us and through us?

Making room for God means that He uses what He puts in our hands. "'Open the east window...shoot...the arrow of the Lord's deliverance and the arrow of deliverance from Syria; for you must strike the Syrians at Aphek till you have destroyed them'" (2 Kings 13:17).

Joash struck the ground only three times, and Elisha said you should have continued to strike the ground because now you will only enjoy partial victory instead of all out victory. God used what Joash gave Him, but more could have been done. This tells us that we are to keep praying, remain faithful, do the small things, or whatever else God asks of us until we see a complete breakthrough and not to give up too soon.

God desires to do something large in us and through us that captures our hearts, our imagination and our future. It doesn't take a lot for God to use it—only our willingness and desire to be used by Him. For Joash, it was a bow and arrow that was to be shot out the window at a given target. The Lord gives us windows of opportunity as we co-labor with Him to bring the kingdom of God to a present reality. God wants to release something in us and through us that is powerful, transformational, and that demonstrates His glory.

We find these truths God wanted to release in and through Joash:

- God says, "I want to do something larger in you than you presently believe."
- God says, "I want to do something in you that gives you greater vision than you presently have."
- God says, "I want to show you that My unmerited favor can work on your behalf."

Why is it important to stay open to the things God puts in our hand like Joash was asked to do with the bow and arrow?

We find other examples of something that was put into someone's hand:

- David collected five smooth stones to kill the giant (1 Samuel 17:40).
- Moses was given a staff that contained the power of God (Exodus 4:2).
- Samson fought the enemy with the jawbone of a donkey and killed a thousand men (Judges 15:15).

- God told Gideon to blow a ram's horn to defeat the enemy, "Then the Spirit of the Lord took possession of Gideon. He blew a ram's horn as a call to arms..." (Judges 6:34, NLT).

Making room for God means we do not stop short of our destiny in Christ. Don't quit too soon. "'Take the arrows...strike the ground;' so he struck three times, and stopped...'You should have struck five or six times'" (2 Kings 13:18-19). Joash would only enjoy partial victory in fighting the enemy. He did enough to get by. Half-way commitment always produces half-way results. Jacob on the other hand said, "I will not let You go unless You bless me" (Genesis 32:26).

We can make these four observations:

- The King lacked passion in overcoming the enemy. He stopped short of having full victory.

- The King took lightly the encouraging word of Elisha. He only did enough to get by.

- The King left undone what he should have completed. Stopping short only leaves those who follow us a greater work to do that should have been done earlier.

- The King could not believe larger than he presently believed. Faith is spelled RISK. God has called us to be people of vision and to pray large prayers that only He can answer.

Making room for God means He will give us strategies for living an overcoming life. Making room for God means He will put something in our hand (in us) that He can use for His glory. Making room for God means don't stop short of our victory. Making room for God is our choice to believe with God all things are possible.

Record your prayer for this lesson:

Group Discussion and Application

Sharing:

How did it go this week? (A time of informal sharing)

Opening prayer inviting the Holy Spirit to guide your time together

Walking Through the Lesson:

- Take time to review the lesson for this week and go over any questions that the group members might have.
- Describe one thing you learned from this lesson.
- What does it mean that God wants to pass on something to us that is powerful and life changing?
- What does it mean for God to take us into His hands and to use us?
- Why do you think we need to be filled with the Holy Spirit according to Luke 24:49?

- What does it mean to co-labor with God in bringing the kingdom of God to a present reality?

- Why was it important for King Joash to keep hitting the ground with his arrows? Why do you think he stopped?

- What made Jacob's statement in Genesis 32:26 so powerful? What does this say to us about how we are to pray and believe God for the breakthrough we need?

- How or in what ways are you going to apply this lesson to your life?

Our Four Commitments:

- To complete the lesson for each week and be ready to share what you learned.
- To let someone in the group know if you are unable to attend the meeting.
- To pray for one another on a regular basis.
- To ask God what He is calling you to do about making disciples through building relationships, reaching out to others, and multiplying through small groups.

BIBLIOGRAPHY FOR SECTION TWO

Barna, George, ***Growing True Disciples***. Colorado Springs, CO: Waterbrook Press, 2001.

Rutland, Mark, ***Launch Out Into the Deep.*** Wilmore, KY: Bristol Books, 1987.

Teykl, Terry, ***The Presence-based Church.*** Muncie, IN: Prayer Point Press, 2003.

Slaughter, Michael ***Unlearning Church.*** Loveland, CO: Group Publishing, 2002.

Wills, Dick, ***Waking to God's Dream***. Nashville: Abingdon Press, 1999.

ABOUT THE AUTHOR

RAY PETTY has served in pastoral ministry for over 37 years. He has pioneered and pastored churches, taught in Bible schools, directed Christian education, and organized life-changing small groups across the Southeast United States. Pastor Ray has been personally impacted by small group ministry and focuses on this solid way to develop disciples, grow leaders, and multiply the church. He is the author of ***Journey In Discipleship Study Guide*** and ***Teach Us to Pray Study Guide***. He received his Masters of Divinity from Asbury Theological Seminary and his bachelors degree from Oral Roberts University. Ray is a husband, father, and grandfather; he lives in Virginia with his wife Alice.

Contact Information

For speaking engagements or special book orders, contact:

Pastor Ray Petty
RayPetty@hotmail.com